*HOW TO LIVE—AND DIE—WITH
MARYLAND PROBATE*

Edited by
J. Nicholas Shriver, Jr.
Shale D. Stiller
Maryland State Bar Association

How to Live– And Die–With Maryland Probate

Here is a comprehensive
treatment of how every Marylander
can save money, time and taxes

Gulf Publishing Company
Houston, Texas

HOW TO LIVE–AND DIE–WITH MARYLAND PROBATE

ISBN 0-87201-512-2
Library of Congress Catalog
Number 73-184684

Preface

The law of probate—the law dealing with the passing of property upon the death of an individual to his family or other beneficiaries—is centuries old, but not fully understood. The purpose of probate, the people it protects, and the advantages it offers should be understood by the ordinary citizen, so that with this understanding he may be able to plan his estate to achieve the purpose of probate, its protections and advantages.

To make known to thoughtful residents of Maryland the basic concepts of probate and the considerable benefits of proper estate planning and use of probate, the Section of Estate and Trust Law of the Maryland State Bar Association has undertaken the publication of *How to Live—and Die— With Maryland Probate.*

Probate often involves federal tax laws, and those are applied generally throughout the United States. Death taxes (and Maryland has them, too) are not only inescapable, but they are also extremely onerous and should be understood by all. Probate also concerns local law, so Maryland residents should find this book of particular value.

The reader will find that probate today is quite obviously not probate as it was in the days before the federal estate tax was devised. Probate today is mostly a problem of tax reporting and tax paying. This has given rise to a science that was mostly unheard of before the American people realized that the federal government, which takes a large share of their earnings during life, accompanies them when they die and is engaged in an ever-increasing struggle to take whatever they leave behind.

As a reading of this book will disclose, there are frequently many very important assets that pass by reason of death on which a will has no effect whatever, and yet these must be carefully considered when reviewing the assets of an estate and making a plan for their disposition. The primary purpose of estate planning is to pass as much property as possible from the dead to the living, or, in proper cases, to charity.

Among nonprobate assets that must be considered by the estate planner are, in most cases, the proceeds (which can be very substantial) of pension and profit-sharing plans, life insurance and joint bank accounts. A person may be entitled by a will of someone who has already died to exercise what is known as a power of appointment. Some of these assets may be subject to federal and state taxes and some may not; a lot depends on the particular facts.

Estate planning can change the amount of taxes payable by a family and whether taxes are payable in the estate of the first or the last spouse to die.

The science of estate planning has been responsible for myriad books and treatises, many of which are written by people who have very little expertise in the subject but who nevertheless purport to give "tax advice" on this complex subject. Therefore, it seems appropriate to add a word of caution. Estate planning is extremely important, but if the people who talk about estate planning emphasize taxes *first*, the listeners had better beware. The primary role of one who plans an estate, and this is ultimately the lawyer, is to ascertain the desires of his client. When the client's wishes are fully understood, and only then, should consideration be given to the tax impact. Thereafter the effort should be to minimize taxes to the fullest degree possible, but never to the extent of overriding the prevailing intent of the client. Monstrosities of wills and distortions of estate plans have appeared on many occasions, and the source can frequently be found to have been an over-zealous "estate planner" who thought first and last of taxes, and who made taxes the paramount consideration in his "estate planning."

Every effort has been made to interpret in this book, fully and fairly, major facets in probate so that the subject can be presented in a well-balanced and readable form. Obviously we do not intend to present a do-it-yourself substitute for carefully made estate plans. On the contrary, the book indicates the folly of homemade wills and of amateur decisions about probate. General principles have been stated to provide an overall view of the subject. Since we are writing for the general reader, certain exceptions to general rules have been omitted. The authors felt that the reader should have an understanding of general principles unencumbered by exceptions.

The Section of Estate and Trust Law of the Maryland State Bar Association expresses its gratitude to the State Bar of Texas and especially to Charles A. Saunders of Houston, Texas, the general editor of *How to Live—and Die--With Texas Probate*, for permission to draw freely upon the Texas publication. Thanks also go to Harold Boucher and Luther Avery of San Francisco, and to the Bar Association of San Francisco, for their work in a similar publication about California law.

With deep gratitude, the Section of Estate and Trust Law of the Maryland State Bar Association acknowledges the work of the following Maryland lawyers who have cooperated, both by writing and editing, in the preparation of this book. Without their thorough, enthusiastic and energetic effort this task could never have been completed.

Albert S. Barr, III, Baltimore
Winston T. Brundige, Baltimore
Clayton C. Carter, Centreville
Mannes Greenberg, Baltimore
John H. Herold, Baltimore
Edward D. Higinbothom, Bel Air

Daniel H. Honemann, Baltimore
W. Jerome Offutt, Frederick
Albin M. Plant, Baltimore
Roger D. Redden, Baltimore
Honorable David Ross, Baltimore
Eugene H. Schreiber, Baltimore
H. Donald Schwaab, Baltimore
Rourke J. Sheehan, Rockvilie
William A. Snyder, Jr., Baltimore
Melvin J. Sykes, Baltimore
Robert M. Thomas, Baltimore
George E. Thomsen, Baltimore
G. Van Velsor Wolf, Baltimore

The Section of Probate and Trust Law of the Maryland Bar Association, from the state that is rightly called America in Miniature, is privileged to present this book as an encouragement to other surrounding states to do the same. We lawyers and citizens of Maryland are proud of our heritage, of the accomplishments of our palatinate-state with our common law traditions, and we are aware of the leadership of our state in the field of legal reform. Maryland was the first state to adopt, even before it was completed, the substance of the Uniform Probate Code, drafted by the Commissioners on Uniform State Laws in cooperation with the Section of Real Property, Probate and Trust Law of the American Bar Association, and now being considered for adoption by many other states. Through its laws, its industry, its freedom—it has not been called the Maryland Free State merely in jest—its citizens share a privilege not easily taken away. In this book we explain to the readers the system under which Maryland, an enlightened jurisdiction, has tried to become as advanced as any state in the Union in its probate laws. We submit that it is a good state in which to live, and to die.

It is most fitting that this book be dedicated to its readers in the hope that they will profit from the material we hereby respectfully submit.

Our thanks to Mrs. Barbara Leasure and Mrs. Mildred Campion for their competent and willing assistance in completing the manuscript.

J. Nicholas Shriver, Jr.
Shale D. Stiller
March 1, 1972
General Editors

Section of Estate and Trust Law
Maryland State Bar Association

Officers

W. Jerome Offutt, Chairman	Frederick
H. Donald Schwaab, Chairman-Elect	Baltimore
Albin M. Plant, Vice-Chairman, Organization	Baltimore
John H. Herold, Vice-Chairman, Estates	Baltimore
Robert M. Thomas, Vice-Chairman, Trusts	Baltimore
Doris P. Scott, Vice-Chairman, Trusts	Elkton
Michael R. Roblyer, Vice-Chairman, Legislation	Annapolis
Albert S. Barr, Secretary	Baltimore

Council Members at Large

Winston T. Brundige	Baltimore
Clayton C. Carter	Centreville
William B. Dulany	Westminster
Daniel H. Honemann	Baltimore

Former Chairmen

G. Van Velsor Wolf	Baltimore
George D. Hubbard	Baltimore
Roger D. Redden	Baltimore
J. Nicholas Shriver, Jr.	Baltimore
Shale D. Stiller	Baltimore

Contents

HOW TO LIVE—AND DIE—WITH
MARYLAND PROBATE

1
What Is
My Probate Estate?

The original meaning of the word *probate* was *test* or *prove.* This word has come to mean the procedure of establishing, before a court of proper jurisdiction, that an instrument is the last will and testament of a deceased person. In Maryland the court in which a will is proved, or probated, is the Orphans' Court, and probate has generally come to include not only the proving of the will but also all of those things that need to be done in connection with estate settlement.

Probate proceedings involve determining whether the deceased has left a valid will; appointing and qualifying a personal representative to settle the estate; collecting the assets of the estate; establishing and paying claims; selling property to pay debts and taxes, or to facilitate distribution of the estate; determining those who are entitled to receive the property of the estate and distributing their property to them; settling the accounts of the personal representative; closing the estate and discharging the personal representative; and all other acts and proceedings in connection with the probate estate.

In Baltimore City and each county (except Montgomery County) probate jurisdiction is exercised by an Orphans'

Court, which is comprised of three judges who are elected for terms of four years. In Montgomery Court a Circuit Court judge exercises all of the jurisdiction of the Orphans' Court in other counties.

The clerical officer responsible for custody of wills and other probate documents and for maintaining records of probate proceedings is the Register of Wills. Again, with the exception of Montgomery County, where the Clerk of the Circuit Court performs the functions of the office of Register of Wills, each county and Baltimore City has a Register of Wills who is also elected for a four-year term.

What Is a Personal Representative?

The personal representative of the decedent's estate is the person authorized by the court to act for the estate. He is appointed by the court and qualifies by filing a statement of acceptance of the duties of the office and by giving bond if it is required. Banks and trust companies as well as individuals may act in this capacity. "Personal representative" is a new designation in Maryland and covers both the old office of executor, the person named in the will to settle the estate and the administrator, the person appointed by the court to settle the estate if there is no will.

The court will appoint the person named in the will unless some unusual reason compels a different appointment. The personal representative must file a bond unless the deceased has directed otherwise in his will or unless bond is excused by written waiver of all persons who legally have an interest in the estate. Even where the testator or the interested parties have excused the posting of a bond, the register, or the court, must require a nominal bond in an amount sufficient to secure payment of all Maryland death taxes payable to the state, and the decedent's debts. No bond is required if a bank is the only personal representative.

After the filing of the personal representative's approved bond, the Register of Wills completes the appointment of the personal representative by issuing a certificate. The certificate is a printed form in which the Register of Wills states that the holder is in charge of the estate and is entitled to possess the assets. This certificate is evidence of the personal representative's authority to take control and possession and to dispose of and distribute the estate's assets.

Estate, Probate Estate and Gross Estate

A person's estate, in the most general sense of the word, includes everything he owns. In this sense, it is the aggregate of all his assets, riches and fortune and includes rights to receive income from property owned by another.

The probate estate of a deceased person is that part of his property and assets which the personal representative of his estate administers and which is subject to the applicable laws and terms of the will and control of the court. The probate estate of a deceased person exists from his death until all debts and taxes have been paid, the property has been distributed, and the personal representative has been discharged. It does not include any property or assets of the deceased which do not pass into the hands of the personal representative. In Maryland, real estate, as well as other forms of property, are included in the probate estate, depending (as in the case of any other property) on the form of ownership at the time of the deceased's death.

For tax purposes the gross estate consists of all property of the decedent which is required to be reported as part of the decedent's gross estate on the federal estate tax return, whether or not the property is part of the probate estate.

The probate estate does not include all property and assets owned by a deceased person during his lifetime. A deceased person may have owned or controlled property or enjoyed income from property during his lifetime which is a part of his gross estate for tax purposes but which is not a part of his probate estate. Even a person of modest means usually owns property which is in fact a part of his estate but which does not pass under his will and never falls into his probate estate. Assets which may not be in the probate estate are described in the following sections.

Insurance

Life insurance is payable on a person's death in the manner provided by the policy. It is usually made payable to a beneficiary other than the estate of the insured, and in case of the prior or simultaneous death of the beneficiary, it is usually made payable to a contingent beneficiary. The insured is usually the owner of the policy. When proceeds of such a policy are not payable to the personal representative of the insured person's estate they do not become a part of his probate estate. However, they will be a part of the probate estate if they are made payable to the insured person's estate by the terms of the policy or if all named beneficiaries die before the proceeds become payable. Moreover, if there are no named and qualified primary or contingent beneficiaries and if the insured owns the policy, the proceeds would be payable to his estate.

Annuities and Employee Benefits

Annuities, pensions and employee benefits usually are not included in the probate estate. An annuity may be payable under what is known as an annuity contract or under an insurance policy with provisions for payment of benefits during the lifetime of the insured and, perhaps, thereafter. An individual may be beneficiary of an annuity created by a contract purchased by him or purchased by another for him. He may be an employee of a corporation which had a pension or profit-sharing plan under which he and his spouse or dependents are entitled to payments. In most cases any amounts payable after the death of the beneficiary will be paid according to the terms of the annuity contract, insurance policy or pension or profit-sharing plan. The amounts payable after the death of the beneficiary do not become a part of his probate estate.

Social Security and Other Government Benefits

Social Security, veteran's benefits and pensions payable under federal law after death do not become a part of the probate estate. However, any amounts payable by law prior to the beneficiary's death are part of his probate estate and are payable as such to his personal representative.

Property in Joint Tenancy

Property owned by the deceased and another in joint tenancy with right of survivorship is not a part of the probate estate. This property is often referred to as *joint tenancy.* Property held in the names of husband and wife is presumed to be held by them as *tenants by the entireties*, which is similar to joint tenancy with right of survivorship. Joint tenancy and entireties property passes to the surviving joint tenant or spouse upon the death of the deceased by operation of law. Stocks, bonds, bank accounts, savings and loan accounts and some other properties are frequently owned jointly or by the entireties. Probably the most common form of property held as tenants by the entireties is the family home. The deed or other instrument of title (such as a savings account pass book) is the usual manifestation of a joint tenancy or a tenancy by the entireties. Jointly owned property is part of the gross estate of a deceased joint owner for tax purposes if the decedent furnished the consideration for the acquisition of the property.

Trust Property

Property conveyed by an individual to a trustee to be administered in trust and distributed after the individual's death usually is not a part of the probate estate. A person has the right to convey his property to a trustee to be held and administered in trust, with the income and property of the trust estate to be used and distributed as provided in the instrument. The grantor may (but usually does not) make himself the trustee; he may reserve the right to alter, amend or revoke the trust during his lifetime; and he may make himself the beneficiary of the trust. The property of a trust of this kind generally would not be subject to administration by his personal representative and therefore would not be a part of his probate estate, unless the trust terminated or was revoked by the grantor prior to his death. In some cases the trust property would be subject to the payment of the decedent's debts.

. If the deceased was the trustee or beneficiary of a trust created by some other person, or if he was entitled to receive income from or use of property, these rights terminate upon his death. The property in which he had these rights will not be part of the probate estate, except income payable to him before death or possibly other vested rights he had in the property at the time of his death.

Trust assets are frequently part of a decedent's gross estate for tax purposes although not part of the probate estate if, for example, the decedent during his lifetime reserved the right to alter or amend the trust, to control the beneficial enjoyment of the assets, or to receive trust income.

U. S. Bonds

United States savings bonds may be made payable to the deceased, a co-owner or to a beneficiary named by the decedent. If the co-owner or named beneficiary survives the deceased, the survivor is the absolute owner of the bonds.

They do not become a part of the decedent's probate estate, although they may be included, in whole or in part, in his gross estate for federal tax purposes. Of course, these bonds will be a part of the surviving co-owner's or named beneficiary's probate estate if he still owns them at the time of his death and has not caused them to be reissued to himself as a co-owner or to a named beneficiary.

Gifts in Contemplation of Death

A person facing imminent death because of advanced age or serious illness cannot reduce his estate taxes by giving property away shortly before he dies. Such a gift, called a gift in contemplation of death, will not take the property out of the donor's gross estate for estate tax purposes. A gift within three years of death is presumed to be in contemplation of death, but the presumption is rebuttable; that is, if evidence shows that the gift was not made in contemplation of death but for other reasons, the property will not be included in the donor's gross estate for federal tax purposes.

Property Conveyed by Decedent in Which He Reserved Income or Control During Life

Even if a decedent gave away property without any thought of death, the property will be included in his gross estate for tax purposes if he reserved income or control over the property during his lifetime. For instance, if the decedent, many years before his death, made a deed gift of real estate to a child, reserving only a life estate to himself, the entire property is included in the decedent's gross estate for tax purposes.

Summary

Not everything a person owns or considers his property will end up as a part of his probate estate. Large parts of the estate often go to beneficiaries outside the will. Care then should be taken to make certain either that a sufficient amount of property (probate estate) will pass under the will to pay estate debts, take care of legacies and accomplish the purposes intended by the will, or else the intention of the testator may very well be frustrated.

2

When Is My Estate Valued and Why?

Post mortem valuation of one's estate will be mandatory. The only general exception under Maryland and federal laws is where the aggregate value of one's estate at the time of death is clearly less than $60,000 and consists entirely of property held jointly with a surviving spouse and/or insurance proceeds designated for a named beneficiary.

The primary reasons why one's estate must be valued after death are

1. To determine the federal estate tax payable by the estate if it exceeds, after all allowable deductions, $60,000 in value on the date of death or the alternate valuation date. (The alternate valuation date is briefly discussed at the end of this chapter.) There is also a Maryland estate tax if the estate exceeds $100,000 in value after all deductions.

2. To determine the state inheritance taxes due upon the transfer of the estate's assets to the beneficiaries of the estate.

3. To help determine what estate assets can and should be sold to raise the cash required to pay taxes, expenses of estate administration, and debts owing at the time of death

and to meet other obligations or requirements which may exist such as supporting a surviving spouse or children during the administration period.
4. To determine what assets might be distributed to legatees and other beneficiaries of the estate in order to satisfy bequests.

Valuation of Assets During Lifetime

The personal representatives (executors or administrators) have certain limited options after death concerning the time at which the value of an estate is to be determined, the method of paying the taxes due and the manner of making distributions to the beneficiaries. However, during his lifetime the testator is in the best position, of course, to take full advantage of those various means available to assure the most economical and efficient transfer of assets to his beneficiaries, free of the encumbrances which could be imposed on his estate if it is not sufficiently liquid to pay his debts and death taxes.

Designing during one's lifetime a pattern for the most economical and efficient transfers of assets to those intended to be the recipients is the essence of proper estate planning. Such planning should be undertaken by almost everyone, regardless of whether he considers his estate large or small.

To design a reasonably satisfactory, workable plan which will achieve the results desired by the testator, it is necessary to value realistically the assets owned at the time. Only by valuing assets can the cash requirements of the estate be determined to ensure satisfaction of debts, final expenses, funeral expenses, administration expenses, taxes and the like. Only by valuing such assets can the testator and his lawyer determine which assets can or should be transferred to specific distributees and what assets or what amounts will remain for distribution.

Circumstances do change and, therefore, an estate plan designed at a given time may not be suitable at a later date. Accordingly, whenever there is a change in a person's circumstances—such as the birth of a child or grandchild, the acquisition of any real property subject to an encumbrance, the acquisition of a business or an interest therein, the embarkment by a child upon an extended, specialized course of education—one's estate plan should be reviewed, and such a review necessitates a revaluation of the assets then owned. As a matter of good policy, an estate plan should be reviewed at least every two to five years. These valuations of assets, made during the owner's lifetime, are the most important valuations of his estate, since only by making them can he properly seek to provide for the cost of transmitting his estate to his beneficiaries. Only at such times can he learn what should be done with the specific assets of his estate, and only then can he decide with some confidence what is to be done with his property. Only by means of these revaluations can the owner revise his plans as changes in circumstances may dictate. Only upon such valuations and revaluations can the testator determine the extent to which his properties will provide income for his widow, furnish an education for his children, or provide the means of carrying out any other intentions.

Some persons may desire to make lifetime transfers of certain assets. A contemplated lifetime transfer is another occasion for valuing one's personal assets. First, and most important perhaps, there should be a general determination as to whether the assets remaining in the donor's ownership and control after such gifts will be sufficient to leave him (or him and his wife) with adequate means of support and security for later years. Secondly, the subject of the contemplated gift must be valued to determine if the transfer would bring gift tax consequences. Thirdly, it is important to consider the death tax exposure of the donor and the extent by which the gift may reduce this exposure. (Of course it must also be determined whether the gift is really the right thing for the intended beneficiary; see Chapter 15).

A person's failure to design a reasonable estate plan during his lifetime and to implement that plan with a proper will and other documents—including the proper registration of ownership of real and other property, proper designation of insurance policy beneficiaries—does not mean that he dies without an estate plan. It means that such a person dies *with* an estate plan imposed upon him by the Maryland laws of descent and distribution, by general principles of law applicable in these instances, and by the judgments and decisions which his personal representative may have to make within the limited options available to him. The estate plan imposed by the State more often than not brings some hardships on the beneficiaries and at least some results which would not have been intended by the testator had he taken time during life to think about the ultimate disposition of his material worth.

Valuation for State Inheritance Taxes, Fixing
Personal Representatives' Commissions, etc.

The Maryland Probate Code requires the personal representative of an estate, within three months after his appointment, to prepare an inventory of the property owned by a decedent at the time of his death, listing each item and indicating its fair market value as of the date of death, together with the type and amount of any encumbrance. Such inventory must include all real estate; all tangible personal property, excluding wearing apparel (other than furs and jewels) and family food items; corporate stocks; debts owed to the decedent, including bonds and notes; bank accounts and the like; and any other interest in property, tangible or intangible, owned by the decedent which passes as a part of his probate estate.

The value of each item listed in the inventory is required to be fairly appraised as of date of death. Corporate stocks listed on a national or regional stock exchange, debts owing to the decedent (other than debts owed by the personal representative to the decedent) and bank accounts may be appraised by the personal representative. All other assets included in the inventory of the decedent are appraised, at the election of the personal representative, either by independent appraisers selected by him or by appraisers regularly employed by the Register of Wills and constituting part of his staff (called standing appraisers under the Probate Code), or by general, independent appraisers appointed by the Register of Wills upon application of the personal representative. The option as to which type of appraiser to use is with the personal representative; but, of course, any appraiser selected by him or pursuant to his request by the Register of Wills must be qualified and disinterested. (In some states the use of court-appointed political appraisers, sometimes of questionable competence, is mandatory, and some are said to charge fees which are unconscionable. This is not so in Maryland.)

The Maryland Probate Code provides that the state, the personal representative or any other interested party may at any time before the estate is closed petition the Orphans' Court for a revision of any value assigned to inventory items, and the court may require such revisions as it deems appropriate. Those estates which are subject to federal estate tax liability often remain open for several years until the federal estate tax return is audited and the federal estate tax liability is finally determined, either by agreement with the Internal Revenue Service or through litigation. Theoretically, therefore, assets in these larger estates could be revalued at any time during the period that the estate is awaiting closing pending the outcome of the federal estate tax determination. However, as a practical matter, the only instance in which a revision in the value of an inventory item would be made is if there has been a very substantial decrease in the value of an asset with an easily ascertainable market value at a given date, such as a listed security, and if that asset is to be transferred to the distributees of the estate in kind. In all other cases, a revision in values of inventory items in large estates is usually of little consequence because (1) increases or decreases in assets which are sold during administration are automatically taken into consideration in the required court accounting, and (2) because of the correlation between the state inheritance and the state and federal estate tax laws, a decrease in inheritance tax would in many cases cause a corresponding increase in the Maryland estate tax.

Whenever any property was not included in the original inventory which is required to be filed within three months from the appointment of the personal representative or whenever the personal representative learns that the value of any asset included in the original inventory was erroneous or misleading, the personal representative is required to file a supplemental inventory showing the correct market value as of the date of the decedent's death of the additional or erroneously appraised items.

The inventory filed by the personal representative and the valuation of the assets contained therein furnish the basis on which he must account to the creditors and beneficiaries to demonstrate proper management of the estate, the payment of claims, the satisfaction of all bequests and devises and the payment of the inheritance tax due to the State of Maryland on the property distributed to the legatees and other beneficiaries. Except where the property of a decedent which is subject to administration in the Orphans' Court has a value of $2,000 or less (and is administered as a so-called small estate), the value of property remaining in an estate after the payment of final lifetime expenses, administration costs, debts and taxes is subject to the Maryland inheritance tax. The rate is 1% for the portions of the estate distributed to one's spouse, lineal descendants, father and mother, and 7½%

for property passing and distributed to other persons (excluding charities, which pay no inheritance tax). No inheritance tax is payable on the small estate, which is referred to above. The details of the Maryland inheritance tax are more fully explained in Chapter 5.

The valuations contained in the inventory filed by the personal representative also serve as the basis for computing commissions to which the personal representative is entitled. Such commissions, as is more fully explained in Chapter 21, are fixed by the Orphans' Court. Further, the inventory values may serve as a basis for the court's requiring an increase in the penal amount of the surety bond where one is required.

The reference above to the payment of inheritance tax merely dealt with such tax which is payable in respect to distributions made to beneficiaries out of one's probate estate—assets which are legally titled in the owner's name only are therefore subject to administration and distribution only by Orphans' Court proceedings. In addition to his probate estate, the decedent may own other types of assets at the time of his death which are subject to a state inheritance tax, namely, property jointly held with persons other than one's spouse and property placed in trust by the owner during his lifetime, with the retention of an interest in such property. In both cases, the property automatically passes to the surviving persons having an interest therein, thus bypassing the probate estate proceedings. However, since an interest passes upon the death of a joint tenant or of the person creating such trust, an inheritance tax is payable to the state upon his death. Accordingly, the jointly held property or the property remaining in such trust must be valued as of the time of death of a joint tenant, in case of property jointly held, or at the death of the creator of the type of trust mentioned above. These valuations must be reported to the Orphans' Court (or the Equity Court if it has assumed jurisdiction over distribution of the property in any such trust) for the imposition of the inheritance tax due.

Valuation for Federal and Maryland Estate Taxes

If a decedent dies after December 31, 1970, his estate must file a federal estate tax return within nine months from the date of death. Each asset or item of property owned by the decedent at the time of his death (with a few, very particularized exceptions) must be reported on this return, together with the value of each asset. The personal representative can elect to value these assets either as of the date of death or as of six months from date of death, the latter date commonly referred to as the alternate valuation date. If a personal representative has not been appointed for a decedent's estate, as for example, where all of his property consisted of jointly held property, the person in actual or constructive possession of the decedent's property must file the federal estate tax return and has the option to select the alternate valuation date.

The alternate valuation date is generally used where there has been a rather sharp, substantial decline in the value of assets, although this alternate valuation date might also be used in smaller estates where there has been an increase in the value of the assets and it may therefore be expedient to pay a little higher estate tax in order to acquire a higher income base for the property. Careful comparison of the estate tax rates of the estate and the income tax rate of the distributees will determine whether to use the higher or lower estate tax valuation. (The proper use of the election might likewise determine whether any federal taxes are due on the estate.)

In any event, the alternate valuation date may be used only if there is a timely filing of the final federal estate tax return, and then the alternate valuation date is used for all property, subject to the following exceptions: If the alternate valuation date is used, then any property distributed, sold, exchanged or otherwise disposed of within the six-month period is valued as of the date of disposition. Secondly, the value of any interest which is affected by a mere lapse of time, such as the paying out of an annuity or the expiration of a patent, is not entitled to be revalued where the revaluation reflects only the effect of the passage of time.

The valuations spoken about here, as well as in the case of state inheritance taxes, are the fair market values of the assets involved as of the applicable valuation date. Often, as with real estate and closely held businesses, it is difficult to determine fair market values—defined generally under the federal estate tax regulations as the price at which a seller is willing to sell and a buyer is willing to buy. For the federal estate tax, the personal representative usually employs qualified appraisers of his own choosing to make a fair market valuation of real estate, and possibly of interests in closely held businesses. If litigation ensues, these appraisers would be available to testify on behalf of the estate and in support of their appraisals. The Internal Revenue Service likewise may employ other independent appraisers or use its own staff of appraisers to determine whether the valuations made on behalf of the estate are "in line" and to testify on behalf of the government's valuation of the assets if litigation on the valuation issue ensues.

Since for federal estate tax purposes at least, uncertainty often exists as to whether the Internal Revenue Service will challenge the estate's valuation of any particular asset, it may be expedient, whenever circumstances permit, for a person during his lifetime to enter into a binding agreement for the sale of a particular asset to be effected upon his death. This device is often used in case of closely held corporations. As an example, let's assume that A and B are the sole stockholders of Corporation X. A and B and Corporation Z enter into an agreement whereby the corporation agrees to purchase the stock of either A or B, whichever is first to die, at a fixed price or, more usually, a price determined in accordance with a fixed formula. If A and B have reached this agreement through arms length bargaining and neither can, by reason of the terms of the contract, sell his stock during their joint lives, then the price payable under the agreement upon B's death for his stock will be binding as the valuation for tax purposes.

The Maryland estate tax is merely a tax equal to the difference between (1) the maximum credit allowable by the federal government as a reduction of the federal estate tax for inheritance taxes paid to Maryland, and (2) the Maryland inheritance taxes paid. Accordingly, the valuation of assets used for federal estate tax purposes will also effectively determine the valuation for Maryland estate tax purposes.

The words of caution set forth in this chapter may be summarized as follows: Since valuation at the end of the line is mandatory, it is wise and prudent in almost every case to make periodic valuations en route so that delivery is insured at the intended destination without undue damage.

3

The Debts I Have Created—How Paid?

In the course of a lifetime every person creates debts. The size and nature of these obligations vary with individual and family situations. It is not surprising that the biggest debts usually are created by the wealthiest people because they have the assets, collateral and credit rating to support larger borrowings. Unfortunately, many families of average means obligate themselves beyond their abilities to pay, causing financial problems during life and most certainly after death. The biggest obligation is usually the mortgage on the home. In addition, there may be innumerable time payments for cars, appliances and other items. In any event, these obligations become a factor to deal with in the administration of an estate.

Take the case of a husband and wife with minor children. If the husband lives to retirement, the mortgage on the home will normally be paid off, along with many other items purchased on credit. But what if the husband dies unexpectedly at an earlier age? He leaves the wife to support the minor children and pay the financial obligations. Further, the main source of income—the husband's earning capacity—is gone. This situation can create quite a hardship on the surviving family members. Therefore, it is the wise man who provides protection for his family in the event of his death.

Provisions in the Will

Many wills provide for the executor to pay debts, taxes and administration costs. Whether or not the will so provides, the personal representative is under a general duty to pay obligations of the decedent's estate. Generally, the debts are paid out of the personal, as distinguished from the real estate, assets of the estate. If the testator desires to insure a different priority, he should say so in his will.

Unless the testator provides that any mortgage or lien which may be outstanding and is secured by any of his property need not be paid by the personal representative, such mortgage or lien may have to be paid out of the residue of the estate. This result might well be contrary to the testator's intention, depriving residuary legatees of sums the testator intended them to have. An attorney drawing a will can avoid this result by specifically providing (if that is what the testator wants) that the personal representative shall not be required to discharge any mortgage or lien by paying a debt prior to maturity; or that the property which is the security for the debt should be used to liquidate the debt (as for example, in the case of a loan on life insurance).

Of course, the important point is that the will should be tailored to the testator's own situation and should state his intentions regarding payment of debts if the statutory scheme is inappropriate. For example, does he wish the home (which usually is held with the wife in a tenancy by the entirety) to pass to the wife burdened with the mortgage or with the mortgage paid?

Funeral Expenses

Occasionally, a testator will include detailed funeral arrangements in his will. If the testator feels strongly about some special funeral arrangements, he should also communicate his feelings to some family member because the will is often not readily accessible at the moment of death.

Funeral expenses and items such as tombstone, grave markers, crypts or burial plots are chargeable against the estate. As a matter of public policy, such expenses are granted a high priority for payment. If the testator has not otherwise provided for their payment in his will, then funeral expenses will be paid out of such assets as are available in the estate. Even if he has what is generally called burial insurance, he should realize that unless he has specifically made such insurance payable to his estate the proceeds may very well not be used to pay for his burial. If prior arrangements regarding the funeral costs have not been made, emotional factors may frequently cause excessive funeral expenses.

It should be noted that unless it is expressly provided in the will that the personal representative may pay such amount for funeral expenses as he deems proper, it may be necessary for the personal representative to obtain an order of court authorizing payment. The court has considerable discretion—although it does not often limit the expenditures—in determining how much of an allowance to authorize for funeral expenses.

Estate and Inheritance Taxes

Just as funeral expenses are an involuntary debt against the estate, so are taxes due because of death. The federal estate taxes and the State of Maryland inheritance taxes may well be, and in many instances are, the largest costs chargeable to the estate. (See Chapters 4 and 5 for a detailed explanation.)

If a person's total property exceeds $60,000, the estate is potentially subject to federal estate taxes. Maryland inheritance taxes are payable even in estates of much smaller size.

It is the personal representative's obligation to pay such taxes as are due. Here again, the testator may have made provisions to satisfy death taxes. And he may have directed in his will what property should be charged with taxes. If not, then the personal representative must look first to any available cash. If there is none, or if the cash is insufficient, he must sell securities or other liquid assets to provide the necessary amount. Failure to provide funds for the payment of taxes may destroy the intention of the testator regarding his beneficiaries. In addition, as previously noted in this chapter, the personal representative may be required to obtain prior approval of the court to sell assets unless there is a properly drawn will.

Many people may not have much cash, but they are wealthy "on paper"; that is, they may own a farm or other assets that are considerably enhanced in value. The father may wish to leave such assets to his wife or children or both. If, at his death, the value of the estate is such that several thousand dollars in taxes are due, then the only alternative may be to sell all or a portion of the assets to raise the necessary funds.

The situation may arise where the testator left sufficient assets to pay all death taxes and other costs and requested that specific bequests be made. For example, the home, personal effects and life insurance proceeds go to the wife; the other real estate to the boys, and stocks and bonds to the daughters. Does the testator intend that each person receive the exact value of each of these assets, or does he intend that such interest bear its proportionate share of death taxes? The will should be clear and explicit with respect to the intention. Under Maryland law, if the will does not clearly direct the payment of death taxes out of the residue of the estate or some other specific source, each person receiving something from the decedent must pay his proportionate share of death taxes.

Planning for Payment of Debts and Taxes

There are steps that may be taken to minimize probate costs, provide for the payment of debts, and reduce estate and inheritance taxes. A few important suggestions are listed here.

1. An up-to-date will, expertly drafted, may clarify many of the problems and, in addition, effect substantial tax savings.

2. A buy-sell agreement funded with life insurance is usually ideal where the testator is a member of a partnership or a closely-held business.

3. A mortgage cancellation life insurance policy on the home assures that the home will pass to the family debt free.

4. Sufficient life insurance to pay all or some debts, costs of probate and taxes helps to make the estate liquid.

5. Investments in other liquid assets that are readily marketable such as stocks, bonds and savings can provide necessary immediate cash.

6. Endowment insurance on the children, designed to mature at the time they are ready for college, will insure future security.

7. Gifts (prior to death) to children or grandchildren, directly or through trusts, give assets to those the testator ultimately wants to provide for. Gifts may also effect substantial tax savings, since the value of the gift reduces the estate for tax purposes.

8. A consistent program of saving also insures future security.

9. Careful selection of a personal representative with knowledge, skill and financial responsibility is always wise and in these days absolutely essential because of the complicated nature of many estates and of the tax laws.

10. Contracting during life for only those obligations that can be paid without financial strain—or providing life insurance to pay them off—will minimize after-death indebtedness.

11. Consideration of educational, religious or other charitable institutions as the ultimate beneficiaries of the estate is particularly appropriate for a family without children. Even though the survivor (husband or wife) may have the benefit of the estate for life, if title rests ultimately in a charity, tax savings may be substantial since gifts to charity are tax free. Thus the debt of taxes is minimized.

Summary

Unchangeable facts of our existence are death, debts and taxes. How debts and taxes are paid after death varies in direct proportion to the thought and planning given to them before death. A person who does not avail himself of the wealth of professional estate-planning talent available today is indeed unwise.

4

Federal Estate Tax

This book has been published because death is inevitable. The federal estate tax, while just as inevitable, can be calculated with precision and substantially reduced—but *only* with careful advance planning.

The federal estate tax is an excise tax imposed upon the transfer of a decedent's property to his beneficiaries—those who share in his assets according to the terms of a will or some other written arrangement or those designated by statute to receive his assets if he dies without a will.

While death itself cannot be avoided, unnecessary donations to the federal treasury can be eliminated. It is the purpose of this chapter to explain, in general terms, the operation of the federal estate tax and some methods for its postponement and reduction.

What Is the Gross Estate?

The starting point in determining federal estate tax is the gross estate. The gross estate consists of the fair market value, at the time of the decedent's death, of all property of all kinds in which the decedent had a taxable interest at the time of his death. The term gross estate is even broader than it seems at first because it also includes, under certain circumstances, property given away by the decedent prior to his death and property subject to his power of disposition even though he may never have owned the property outright. For example, the items listed below may be included in the decedent's gross estate:

1. *Property given away by the decedent during his lifetime.* The value of such gifts will be included in the decedent's gross estate if the gifts were made in contemplation of death—that is, a gift made as a substitute for a testamentary gift with the purpose of avoiding death taxes. A clear example would be a gift by a terminal cancer patient of all of his property to his wife and children shortly after being informed of the nature of his disease. However, no gift which has been completed more than three years prior to the death of the decedent will be included in his gross estate, no matter how much the decedent had tax avoidance as his purpose.

2. *Certain property transfers made by the decedent during his lifetime in which he retained certain rights.* Those forbidden rights include (1) the continued right to possession or enjoyment of the property or the income from it, and (2) the right to designate at a later time those persons who shall subsequently possess or enjoy the property or the income from the property. An example would be the transfer of a house by the decedent to his son where the decedent retained the right to live in the house until his death without paying rent. Another example is where the decedent transfers title to securities to his son, but the decedent in fact gets the dividends.

3. *Transfers taking effect at death.* Such transfers include, for example, one where the ultimate beneficiary or beneficiaries will receive the property only by surviving the decedent, and there is a chance that if the beneficiary died

before the decedent the property would return to the decedent (or be subject to his power of disposition) prior to his death.

4. *Revocable transfers.* Such transfers include "incomplete" transfers where the decedent has the power to alter, amend, revoke or terminate such a transfer. An example would be the decedent's creation of a trust for the benefit of his wife and children with the retention by the decedent of the right to determine which beneficiaries will receive how much income or the right to revoke the trust and return the property to himself. (See Chapter 13 for a more detailed discussion of revocable transfers.)

5. *Jointly owned property.* This includes joint bank accounts as well as securities, real estate or other property owned jointly (with all rights vested in the survivor) or as tenants by the entireties (husband and wife). The value of all such jointly owned property is included in the decedent's estate, except to the extent that the estate can prove that part or all of the purchase price was furnished by the other joint owner or owners. (See Chapter 12 for a more detailed discussion of jointly owned property.)

6. *Property subject to the decedent's power of appointment.* This would include the value of all property which the decedent had the power to transfer, either during his lifetime or at his death, to his estate, his creditors, the creditors of his estate or himself. An example would be property in a trust created by another, if the decedent had the right to terminate the trust and transfer the property to himself, or had the right to direct that the property be transferred to his estate or his creditors at his death. (See Chapter 19 for a more detailed discussion of powers of appointment.)

7. *Life insurance.* All life insurance owned by the decedent is included in the gross estate, regardless of whether the insurance proceeds are payable to a named beneficiary or to the decedent's estate. Furthermore, the gross estate will include the value of life insurance policies owned by others if

the decedent possesses, at the time of his death, the right to borrow on the policy, to change the designation of beneficiaries or *any other* "incidents of ownership" of the policy. (See Chapter 14 for a more detailed discussion of life insurance.)

These examples are by no means exhaustive. They merely serve to indicate the complexity involved in determining just what is included in the decedent's gross estate.

Alternate Valuation

If the personal representative of the decedent's estate so chooses, the gross estate, instead of being valued on the date of the decedent's death, can be valued on a subsequent date which would normally be six months after the decedent's death. All property, however, must be valued either on the date of death or on the alternate valuation date; the personal representative cannot pick and choose and value some assets as of the date of death and other assets six months later. If the personal representative elects the alternate valuation date, then property sold, distributed and otherwise transferred or disposed of between the date of death and six months thereafter is valued on the date of such sale, disposition or transfer. For all other assets the alternate valuation date would be six months after the date of death.

Permitting the personal representative to elect the alternate valuation date helps to eliminate the hardship that would otherwise arise if taxes were calculated on the date of death value and the value of all assets declines while the tax money is being raised.

Deductions

Funeral expenses, debts of the decedent, claims against the decedent's estate, administration expenses (including fees paid to personal representatives and attorneys), certain losses and other such items may be deducted from the gross estate. In addition, the estate may deduct the value of property left to charity and also the value of certain property transferred to the decedent's surviving spouse. This marital deduction is more fully described in Chapter 6.

After all deductions from the gross taxable estate are made, the figure remaining is the net taxable estate. In many instances, this figure will be substantially less than the decedent's gross estate. The federal estate tax is based on this net figure in much the same way as the federal income tax is applied against net taxable income remaining after all deductions.

To find the taxable estate, the net taxable estate as just described is reduced by a $60,000 exemption which is allowable in all cases. This is like the deduction for personal exemptions permitted on income tax returns. This final figure, that is, the taxable estate, is the figure against which the federal estate tax rates are applied.

Tax Rates

The federal estate tax, like the income tax, is a progressive tax. The rates begin at 3% on the first $5,000 of the net taxable estate (after the $60,000 exemption is subtracted) and rise to a maximum of 77% for a net taxable estate exceeding $10,000,000. The increase in rates is rather spectacular. With a net taxable estate of $40,000, the federal estate tax is $4,800; this rises to $9,500 on a net taxable estate of $60,000 and $20,700 on a net taxable estate of $100,000. On a $250,000 net taxable estate, the federal estate tax is $65,000. Table 4-1 shows the rates applicable to taxable estate of various sizes. (See end of this chapter.)

Estate taxation is becoming increasingly burdensome every year, even though Congress has not changed the rates in recent years. This is because the $60,000 exemption from tax was originally enacted in 1942 and has never been changed.

Meanwhile, inflation has been rampant, so that what was a reasonably substantial exemption in 1942 is now a far lesser one, and thousands of people who were not required to pay estate tax are now forced to do so. As dollars have become more plentiful, more and more people who die are forced to have "estates" which are still terribly small in terms of purchasing power but nevertheless are subject to the ruthless federal estate tax.

Credits

After all deductions have been taken and the federal estate tax has been computed, this tax may be reduced by one or more of four allowable credits. Those credits are:

1. *State death taxes.* A credit may be allowed against the federal estate tax for certain estate, inheritance or similar taxes paid to any state or territory or the District of Columbia with respect to property included in the gross estate. The amount of this credit is subject to various limitations, and in many cases—particularly where the Maryland collateral inheritance tax (discussed in Chapter 5) applies—may be far less than the actual inheritance taxes paid. Therefore, assuming that the credit was originally enacted by Congress to encourage the assessment by the various states of some sort of death tax, it certainly has fulfilled its role in Maryland. The Maryland inheritance tax is quite adequate, so that the credit is usually absorbed by the Maryland inheritance taxes. Where it isn't, however, the Maryland estate tax fills the void.

2. *Gift taxes.* If a gift tax has been paid with respect to a gift made by the decedent and if such gift is included in the decedent's gross estate as a gift made in contemplation of death (discussed above), certain portions of the gift tax may be claimed as a credit against the amount of the estate tax.

3. *Prior estate taxes paid.* The decedent's estate may claim a credit for federal estate tax paid by the estate of a prior

decedent with respect to a transfer of property to the decedent before his death. The existence and amount of the credit depends on the time interval between the deaths of the two decedents, provided that the period does not exceed 10 years. The credit is allowable even though the decedent may have sold, given away, otherwise disposed of or lost the property received from a prior decedent.

The purpose of the credit is to prevent excessive erosion of assets that otherwise might result from the unhappy event of successive deaths within a relatively short period of time. The maximum credit is allowed where two deaths take place within two years of each other. Beyond that, the credit must be reduced by 20% every two years. After 10 years, no credit is available with respect to federal estate taxes paid upon the death of the prior decedent. The credit is calculated by an extremely complicated formula which makes certain that only an irreducible minimum of allowance is made for the amount of tax previously paid.

4. *Foreign death taxes.* A credit may be allowed with respect to estate, inheritance or similar taxes paid to foreign governments by the decedent's estate. Such credits are subject, however, to various limitations specified in the Internal Revenue Code and in various treaties between the United States and foreign governments.

Minimizing the Tax

The primary purpose of estate planning is to make sure that the decedent's assets are available for his chosen beneficiaries. The next step should be to find the least expensive way, taxwise, of achieving the desired results. Indeed, proper tax planning can substantially reduce the total estate tax burden even for the next generation.

Gifts during life and the use of trusts—either those created during life or pursuant to the terms of a will—are among the most widely used methods of reducing the impact of federal

Table 4-1
Computation Of Estate Tax
(After deduction of $60,000 exemption)

(A) Taxable estate equal to or more than—	(B) Taxable estate less than—	(C) Tax on amount in column (A)	(D) Rate of tax on excess over amount in column (A)
$ 0	$ 5,000	$ 0	3
5,000	10,000	150	7
10,000	20,000	500	11
20,000	30,000	1,600	14
30,000	40,000	3,000	18
40,000	50,000	4,800	22
50,000	60,000	7,000	25
60,000	100,000	9,500	28
100,000	250,000	20,700	30
250,000	500,000	65,700	32
500,000	750,000	145,700	35
750,000	1,000,000	233,200	37
1,000,000	1,250,000	325,700	39
1,250,000	1,500,000	423,200	42
1,500,000	2,000,000	528,200	45
2,000,000	2,500,000	753,200	49
2,500,000	3,000,000	998,200	53
3,000,000	3,500,000	1,263,200	56
3,500,000	4,000,000	1,543,200	59
4,000,000	5,000,000	1,838,200	63
5,000,000	6,000,000	2,468,200	67
6,000,000	7,000,000	3,138,200	70
7,000,000	8,000,000	3,838,200	73
8,000,000	10,000,000	4,568,200	76
10,000,000	. . . .	6,088,200	77

estate taxes. A pattern of giving, spread out over a period of years, can substantially reduce a decedent's taxable estate under the present gift and estate tax laws, with little or no gift tax payments. A program of *inter vivos* giving, however, never should be undertaken until ample provisions have been made for the decedent's spouse. (See Chapter 15 for a more complete explanation of gifts and their tax effect.)

Another widely used method of reducing eventual estate taxes is to place into a testamentary trust the property that is taxed at the decedent's death. Both the income and the principal of the trust can be made available under certain circumstances to the decedent's designated beneficiaries during their lives. At the death of those beneficiaries, the property can be transmitted to the next generation under present federal laws without the imposition of further estate taxes. While technical requirements relating to such trusts must be met, their use can reduce the overall tax burden even where the size of the estate is relatively moderate. Such trusts are discussed more extensively in the chapters dealing with irrevocable trusts (Chapter 16) and with the marital deduction (Chapter 6).

Paying the Tax

Generally, the estate tax must be paid in cash (or with certain Treasury bonds) nine months after the date of death. Thus, proper estate planning demands that adequate calculation of and provision for the estate's cash needs may result in the personal representative having to raise funds by selling assets during unfavorable market conditions.

Under certain circumstances, the personal representative may be granted an extension of up to 10 years to pay the full estate tax bill. This alternative is available in certain "hardship" cases or if an interest in a closely held business constitutes a substantial portion of the estate.

Summary

The federal estate tax laws are extremely complex. However, with careful planning the impact of federal estate taxes may both be understood and substantially reduced. The available techniques for reducing federal estate tax, when properly used, can conserve additional dollars for ultimate distribution to the decedent's chosen beneficiaries. The opportunities for reduction of taxes have been made available by the Congress. They should not be wasted.

5

Maryland Inheritance Tax

The first Maryland inheritance tax was enacted by the General Assembly in 1844. It was only the second such tax to be adopted in this country, Pennsylvania having adopted one in 1826. Since 1935 such a tax has been imposed on direct inheritances at 1% and on collateral inheritances at 7½%.

The Registers of Wills of the several counties and of Baltimore City are charged with responsibility of collecting this tax, primarily from the personal representatives of the estates being administered in their respective jurisdictions and ultimately from the beneficiaries—the persons who have acquired the property subject to taxation.

This tax is not limited strictly to inheritances and the designations "direct" and "collateral" are somewhat misleading.

Basically, the tax is imposed on the net value of any item of property worth more than $150 which passes as a result of the decedent's death. This includes not only inheritances in the sense of property passing by the laws of intestate succession but also gifts made by a will, jointly owned property passing to a survivor other than a surviving spouse (husband or wife) and most remainder interests passing after the death of a life tenant. Also taxable is property transferred within two years prior to death, which is presumed, subject to contrary proof, to have been given by the donor in contemplation of his death.

If the decedent was a resident of Maryland, taxable property includes personal property regardless of its location, and real property located in Maryland. If the decedent was not a Maryland resident, determining what items of property passing as a result of his death are subject to Maryland inheritance tax is more complex. Generally, any interest in real estate or tangible personal property (such as furniture, jewelry and books) actually located in Maryland is subject to tax, but items of intangible personal property (such as stocks, bonds or insurance policies) owned by a nonresident are not subject to tax even if actually located here at the time of the death.

The direct 1% tax is payable on taxable interests in property passing to the decedent's father, mother, husband, wife, children, grandchildren or more distant lineal decedents. The major exemption from this direct tax is the value of any interest in property passing to a surviving spouse by virtue of a joint tenancy or tenancy by the entireties.

The collateral 7½% tax is payable on taxable interests in property passing to all other beneficiaries, that is, brothers, sisters, nephews, nieces, grandparents, more distant relatives and friends.

Specifically exempt from the tax is property passing to or for the use of any organization whose purposes are exclusively charitable, religious, scientific, literary or educational, including the encouragement of art and the prevention of cruelty to children or animals, provided no substantial part of the organization's activities is directed at propaganda or attempting to influence legislation. In addition, there is a $500 exemption for bequests for the perpetual upkeep of graves.

Also exempt from taxation are the proceeds of life insurance policies payable to anyone other than the decedent-insured's estate.

Unlike the federal estate tax, the Maryland inheritance tax is not imposed on the property a person owns at his death but rather on the "privilege" of others of taking the property when it is distributed to them. Therefore, the tax is computed on the net value of taxable property actually received by the beneficiary at the time he is presumed to receive it. Thus, an heir's inheritance by intestate succession and a beneficiary's bequest under a will are taxable at the time of distribution during the course of administration of the decedent's estate. On the other hand, the decedent's interest in property passing to a joint and surviving co-owner, the value of property passing to a remainderman at the death of a life tenant under a trust or otherwise, and gifts made in contemplation of death are taxable at the decedent's death, although the tax is not actually due until 90 days after death. As a practical matter, however, the valuation date for inheritance tax purposes is almost always the decedent's date of death, regardless of the date of actual receipt of the property.

There is no inheritance tax return as such. With respect to property passing by intestate succession or under a will, the administration account filed in the probate proceedings by the decedent's personal representative which shows distribution of the taxable property serves as the return and reflects the tax which is payable. The tax so shown is paid at the time the account is filed with the Register of Wills. With respect to jointly owned property, remainder interests and gifts in contemplation of death, an "Information Report" disclosing the pertinent information about such property is required to be filed with the Register of Wills within 90 days of the date of death. An "Application to Fix Inheritance Tax" with respect to jointly owned property or remainder interests and a joint account return with respect to joint bank accounts must also be filed within the 90-day period. The Register then calculates, assesses and bills the tax on the basis of the information furnished.

Interest at the annual rate of 6% begins to accrue on inheritance taxes unpaid 30 days after the due date. The applicable statute of limitations bars collection of the tax still unpaid four years after the due date, but inheritance tax due with respect to any interest in real estate is a lien on that interest for a period of at least four years and in some instances 12 years after the date of death. Furthermore, it is not altogether clear in many instances just when the "due date" is. If, as Plato is reported to have said, "only the dead have seen the end of war" then in Maryland as well as many other places, not even the dead have seen the end of taxation.

Maryland Estate Tax

The Maryland estate tax was first imposed in 1929. Its primary purpose is to secure to the state those taxes for which a credit is allowed by the federal estate tax laws to an estate which is subject to federal estate tax to the extent that the credit is not covered by the inheritance taxes paid. It is a "pick-up" tax which picks up for the State of Maryland estate taxes from a federally taxable estate which would otherwise be paid to the federal rather than the state government.

A Maryland estate tax return is due 15 months after death. It must be amended when the federal estate tax return is amended or is changed upon audit or litigation. The tax is payable when the return is filed, and any deficiency and interest is due when an amended return is filed.

The amount of the Maryland estate tax is fixed by the credit which the federal Congress has allowed, but it is determined after deducting state inheritance taxes that have been paid. The tax is payable to the state Comptroller.

Tax on Commissions

As the inheritance tax takes a bite out of the "privilege" of inheritances, so the tax on commissions takes a bite out of the "privilege" of serving as the decedent's personal representative. This tax is imposed at the rate of 1% on the first $20,000 gross value of the probate estate, other than real estate, plus 1/5% on the balance; *or* at the rate of 10% of the total commissions allowed, whichever computation produces—naturally!—the greater tax. Furthermore, the tax is due even if the personal representative waives his rights to receive commissions.

Efforts have been made by the Section of Estate and Trust Law of the Maryland State Bar Association to simplify the Maryland death tax structure, but these efforts have been stalled by the insistence of various state officials upon rates which would vastly increase the revenues from death taxes. Perhaps naively, the lawyers believe that such taxes are already high enough.

6

What Is the Marital Deduction?

If you are married or are contemplating marriage, and if either you or your spouse owns or expects to own any property, the marital deduction can be of vital importance in connection with your estate planning.

History of the Marital Deduction

To understand the marital deduction and how it works, it is helpful to know a little of its history and the reasons Congress enacted it. In about eight states in the western part of the country, known as community property states, half of the property acquired by the spouses during marriage is, generally speaking, owned by each spouse.

Before 1942, upon the death of a spouse in a community property state, only that spouse's half-interest in the community property was subject to the federal estate tax. In the other common law or separate property states, such as Maryland, all or most of the property acquired by a couple during marriage was often the husband's separate property. All such property was taxed on the husband's death, resulting in much higher estate taxes than would have been the case if the husband were, as in the community property states, considered the owner of half the marital estate.

To correct this inequity, Congress first attempted (in 1942) to override the community property laws by taxing the husband's estate as if he owned all of the community property. This law, however, was manifestly unfair to the community property states and was finally repealed in 1948. After 1948, as in the years before 1942, only the decedent's half-interest in the community property is taxable. In the same year, however, Congress enacted the marital deduction to give residents of common law states the same tax treatment given to residents of community property states. This was accomplished by giving the estate of the first spouse to die a deduction for any property left to the surviving spouse. The deduction could be as much as half the value of the decedent's property.

Stated differently, this means that the value of any property left to the surviving spouse is excluded from the decedent's taxable estate to the extent of half of the value of the decedent's total estate. If, for example, the entire estate of a husband and wife in Maryland were considered to be the husband's property, and he died, leaving in his will all of his property to his wife, then only half of his estate would be taxable. This provides the same treatment, if not by the same methods, as in a community property state.

Importance to Maryland Residents

The marital deduction is important to Maryland residents. If property is left to someone other than the surviving spouse, or if it is left to the surviving spouse in a way that the Internal Revenue Code does not permit to receive the marital deduction, the decedent's entire property may be subject to an estate tax. If, however, the property is left to the surviving spouse in such manner as to meet the requirements of the marital deduction law, only half of it will be taxable.

Just how much difference such estate planning can make is shown in the following example. Assume that the husband and wife were recently married and that the husband has a net estate of $300,000. If he dies and his estate does not receive any marital deduction, the federal estate tax would exceed $62,000. If his estate receives the maximum marital deduction, however, the tax would be reduced to approximately $18,000—a saving of some $44,000.

The words "in such manner as to meet the requirements of the marital deduction law" must be emphasized because of their importance. While presented here in simple fashion, application of the marital deduction frequently involves extremely difficult questions of law and complex mathematical computations. For instance, only property which "passes" from the decedent to the surviving spouse can qualify for the marital deduction. Whether particular assets pass properly to the surviving spouse often presents technical problems, and careful planning and drafting is required to insure that the bequest is in the acceptable form. The total amount of the deduction is limited to 50% of the value of the decedent's adjusted gross estate. Determination of the adjusted gross estate is necessary before drafting wills or trust agreements to insure that the estate receives the maximum marital deduction benefits; this determination is sometimes highly involved. The necessary planning and the ultimate answers to these questions are problems for an attorney. The Supreme Court of the United States has observed that "the achievement of the purposes of the marital deduction (remains) . . . dependent to a great degree upon the careful drafting of wills."

It is easier to understand some of the problems involved in applying these statutory tests if we bear in mind the basic purpose of the marital deduction: to place *separate* property and *community* property on an equal footing before the estate tax, so that only half of the separate property will be taxed when left to the surviving spouse. It is not all a gift, however; to qualify for the marital deduction, property must be left to the surviving spouse in such a manner that it *will be taxable* in the estate of the surviving spouse. Usually there is still, however, a dramatic reduction in the total tax.

Property Which Qualifies for the Deduction

All kinds of property interests used to determine the value of the decedent's gross estate for tax purposes may qualify for the marital deduction if passed to the surviving spouse in the proper fashion. As seen previously, such interests include not only the familiar outright bequests of personal and real property to the surviving spouse, but also such interests as transfers made to the spouse during the decedent's lifetime (if made under such circumstances as to be included in the gross estate), proceeds of life insurance payable in the pre-scribed manner to the surviving spouse, and interests passing under a revocable living trust, if properly drawn.

The property must pass to the surviving spouse within the requirements of the Internal Revenue Code. As previously noted, the basic consideration is that the property must be left to the surviving spouse in such manner as to be taxable in the surviving spouse's estate on his or her subsequent death, unless consumed or otherwise disposed of during his or her lifetime. If the surviving wife, for example, is given only a life estate in the property, that is, if the property is bequeathed to her for her lifetime but will pass to someone else upon her death, then it would not be taxable in her estate and does not qualify for the marital deduction. Such interests are generally called terminable interests.

However, the bequest of the life estate can provide that the income from the property be paid to the widow at least annually and that she have the power to direct in her will that the property shall go to her estate upon her death or shall go to others she may designate. In this case the property would be taxable in her estate and therefore qualifies for the marital deduction. This is true even though she fails to exercise the power of appointment, in which event the property would go to those persons alternatively designated in the husband's will. Instead of the power of appointment in her will, she can be given an unrestricted right to appoint the principal to herself during her lifetime or to invade the principal for her own use or other disposition.

The Marital Deduction Trust

These rules permit using a device which provides a desirable and flexible way to take advantage of the maximum marital deduction and at the same time protect the interests of the surviving spouse and carry out the testator's desires as to the disposition of his property. This device is the marital deduction trust.

To understand the workings of such a trust, assume that the husband dies first, leaving a substantial amount of property. He can leave roughly half of his property—the maximum permitted by the marital deduction statute—in a marital deduction trust for his widow for her lifetime. The trustee would be directed to pay all income from the trust to the widow at intervals not less frequently than once a year. (Monthly or quarterly payments may be specified in the will.) The trustee also can be given the power to expend principal of the trust to support the wife (but not anyone else in the family) in such fashion as may be appropriate or to help her in case of illness or other emergencies. These provisions can be completely flexible and may express the desires of the testator, provided that the widow receives all income from the trust at least annually and that, in addition, the trust gives the widow the power to appoint the property, that is, dispose of it in her will to whomever she wishes (or, in the alternative, to appoint or invade the principal during her lifetime without restriction). There cannot be any restrictions on her ability to appoint to anyone—even a second husband.

The trust can further provide that in the event the widow fails to exercise properly the power of appointment, then upon her death the trust will pass to the children or to whomever the testator might select. Normally, the surviving widow would, if she exercised the power at all, exercise it in favor of the couple's children. The existence of the power of appointment affords another—nontax—advantage. The widow, during the years following her husband's death, can observe the children and their needs and make a distribution which, in the light of later circumstances, is more equitable or desirable than that in the husband's will. At the same time, the wife is protected against her own lack of experience in financial matters in that the investment of the trust funds would be controlled by a trustee, and the wife could not reach the principal of the trust except in the instances already mentioned.

The legal requirements of a marital deduction trust can become quite technical. Expert preparation is required, especially in Maryland where the rules with respect to powers of appointment are unique in the United States. Among other limitations there are restrictions on the type and amount of unproductive property which may be included. No single form of trust can be used in all situations—each must be tailor-made to fit the particular estate involved. It should be remembered that the advantages of the marital deduction are equally available to the estate of the wife should she die first, so that if she does die first she can leave up to one-half of her property to or for the benefit of her husband and thus obtain the deduction.

Advantages of a Second Trust

Since in the example we have just used, only half of the husband's separate property can qualify for the marital deduction, it is frequently desirable to create two trusts in the husband's will—a marital deduction trust and a regular trust. Depending upon the size of the estate, family circumstances and other factors, a regular trust can carry out the testator's wishes. The greatest tax savings can be effected by drafting a second trust in a manner that will prevent the principal from being taxed in the surviving wife's estate upon her death. For example, the second trust could provide that the income be paid to the wife during her lifetime and after her death pass to the children or to such other persons as the testator might select. This trust estate would not then be taxed in the surviving wife's estate upon her death because she was only a life beneficiary without any power of appointment.

The ultimate savings accomplished by the use of such multiple trusts can be quite substantial. Assuming again that the husband has a net estate of $300,000, if he leaves his estate outright to his wife or leaves his entire estate in a marital deduction trust, the total federal estate taxes after the property has been taxed first in his estate and a second time in the wife's estate when she dies will be over $71,000. If multiple trusts are properly used, one of which is a marital deduction trust, the total taxes after the deaths of both spouses will be $35,000—a net savings of $36,000.

The Marital Deduction Should Not Be Used in All Cases

Such considerations make it appropriate at this point to inject a word of caution—it is not always desirable to take advantage of a marital deduction. Before the client and his attorney can make an intelligent decision as to using the marital deduction, the effect on the subsequent estate of the surviving spouse must be considered. Under some circumstances the fact that the property qualifying for the marital deduction must necessarily be taxed in the surviving wife's estate may substantially reduce the possible ultimate savings. Family problems, the ages of the spouses, the size of the surviving spouse's own separate estate, income tax problems which might be created by designating the surviving spouse as the income beneficiary, the undesirability in some instances of giving the surviving spouse the unrestricted power of appointment or power to invade principal which would be necessary to qualify for the marital deduction—all of these may in many instances result in a decision not to utilize the marital deduction. The decision can be made only after the client and his attorney have carefully considered all of the circumstances, including the ultimate wishes of the client, the size of the estate and the nature of the assets involved.

7

Gifts to Charity

Gifts to charity play an important role in the financial plans of a great many Marylanders. Generally speaking, people give to a charity primarily because they believe in its cause, and the primary benefit to the giver is usually the fulfillment of a religious obligation, or the sense of satisfaction derived from making the gift.

As a welcome byproduct, many gifts to charity produce significant federal and state tax savings, and these savings sometimes provide important additional benefits. This chapter will not deal with why people make gifts to charity, nor directly with what or how much they can or should give. Instead, it will discuss various ways of making gifts to charity and some of the effects these means of giving have on probate planning.

Outright Gifts Under a Will

A property owner frequently makes a number of outright gifts under his or her will—often called outright bequests. For example, personal and household effects are generally left outright to one or more family members, and cash or other property is often left outright to family members, friends or loyal employees. In addition, many individuals make outright bequests to charitable organizations with which they are connected or in which they are interested.

When a person makes an outright gift under a will to a qualified charity, the bequest generates an unlimited federal estate tax deduction in an amount equal to the value of the gift. Since this charitable deduction applies against the highest tax bracket of the estate, the larger the individual's taxable estate, the greater the economic benefit derived from the charitable deduction.

Many charitable bequests are also exempt from the Maryland inheritance tax and the Maryland estate tax. Furthermore, except for the right of a surviving spouse to his or her statutory share, Maryland law places no limitation on the amount which an individual may leave to charity.

Outright bequests to charity seldom cause probate planning problems. However, where such a gift is planned, the property owner should insure that there will be adequate liquidity in the estate. He must be aware of the need for enough cash, or assets which may readily be converted to cash, to pay (1) taxes, (2) expenses of estate settlement and (3) outright bequests of cash including those to charity.

Charitable Remainder Gifts Under a Will

Quite often, an individual would like to make a substantial gift to charity under his or her will but feels that one or more family members should not be deprived of the income the property will produce. In such a case, a charitable remainder gift under the will often provides an ideal solution. Such a gift reduces federal and state taxes and results in additional funds for the income beneficiaries. It also preserves capital for the ultimate benefit of charity.

Most charitable remainder bequests planned today are made through the use of a trust created under the will. Under present law, if the value of a remainder interest given to charity through a trust under a will is to qualify for a federal estate tax deduction, the trust must be either what is known as a charitable remainder *annuity trust,* or a charitable remainder *unitrust.*

An Annuity Trust

A charitable remainder annuity trust is one which pays out a fixed sum each year, and this amount may not be less than 5% of the initial net fair market value of the property transferred to the trust. As an example, under his will an individual left $100,000 to create a charitable remainder annuity trust. He gave a qualified charity the remainder interest, and he gave his wife, for the rest of her life, the right to receive annual payments amounting to 5% of the value of the property at the time it is transferred to the trust. This is an annuity trust, and regardless of whether the value of the trust principal increases or decreases, the wife will receive $5,000 each year (5% of $100,000).

A Unitrust

A charitable remainder unitrust is one from which a fixed percentage—not less than 5%—of the net fair market value of the trust's assets, valued annually, is to be paid out each year. As an illustration, under her will, an individual created a unitrust with $50,000. She gave the remainder interest to charity, and her sister is to receive, for the sister's lifetime, annual payments equal to 5% of the annual value of the trust's assets. Assume that the assets are valued at $50,000 in the first year, $55,000 in the second year and $60,000 in the third year. In such event, the sister will receive $2,500, $2,750 and $3,000, respectively, in these years. In later years, the sister will continue to receive 5% of whatever the value of the trust property may be in each such year, whether higher or lower than the original amount.

A Variation on the Unitrust

Under an alternate arrangement, a will creating a unitrust can provide that if the actual income is less in any year than the specified percentage, only the actual income need be paid to the beneficiary in such year. In such a case, it will also provide that if the income in any year is less than the specified percentage, the difference will be made up in future years if and when excess income is available.

The Federal Estate Tax Deduction

Where a charitable remainder annuity trust or unitrust is created under a will, the estate is entitled to a charitable deduction for the value of the remainder interest given to charity. For federal estate tax purposes, a charitable remainder trust established under a will actually amounts to two separate gifts. One is a gift to the income beneficiary of the actuarial value of his or her income interest. The other is a gift of the remainder interest to charity.

The value of each of these interests—and, therefore, the amount of the deduction—is determined from tables supplied by the Internal Revenue Service. The keys to such valuation are (1) the value of the property transferred to the trust, (2) the term of the trust and (3) the rate of return that is specified.

Providing Increased Benefits

Because of the estate tax deduction allowed for the gift of a remainder interest to charity, a charitable remainder annuity trust or unitrust can be used to reduce or perhaps even eliminate the federal estate tax. The net effect is to provide greater advantages for both the income beneficiary and the charity.

For example, a bachelor—whose estate, after expenses but before taxes, will amount to approximately $200,000—has for many years been helping to support his mother. He wants to protect his mother, but he also wants to leave as much of his property as possible to a charity in which he is interested. Therefore, his will leaves his entire estate in a charitable remainder annuity trust with a 5% income interest payable to his mother for life. At her death, all of the trust principal will be paid to the charity.

If the bachelor's mother is already over 70 years of age, the combination of the charitable deduction and the $60,000 specific exemption (to which every estate is entitled) will be enough so that his estate will pay little or no federal estate tax. If, instead, he should leave his property outright to his mother with the understanding that she will leave it to the charity at her subsequent death, the gross federal estate tax at his death will amount to $32,700. In such a case, his mother would lose the income from this $32,700, and the charity would ultimately receive its gift less the $32,700.

Combining the Marital and Charitable Deductions

In a large estate, both the marital deduction and a charitable remainder trust can often be used (1) to minimize the federal estate tax, (2) to produce additional funds for the surviving spouse and (3) to preserve capital for the ultimate benefit of charity. For instance, assume the case of a husband who has no children and therefore wants to leave a sizeable portion of his estate to charity but also wants to be sure that after his death his wife will be taken care of adequately the rest of her life.

To accomplish these objectives, he executes a will that takes maximum advantage of the federal estate tax marital deduction. This means that one-half of his adjusted gross estate will escape the federal estate tax if his wife survives him. His wife will receive the income from the property that qualifies for the marital deduction, and all of the principal will be available for her security and protection.

In addition, this man's will leaves the rest of his estate to a charitable remainder unitrust. Five percent of the trust's assets, valued annually, will be paid to his wife for the rest of her life, and at her death the remaining principal of the trust will be paid to the charity.

Under this arrangement, the federal estate tax in the husband's estate will be cut to the bone. One-half of his adjusted gross estate qualifies for the marital deduction. As to the other half, the value of the charitable remainder will be allowed as an estate tax deduction, and only the value of the wife's income interest in the unitrust will be subject to the federal estate tax. As a result of the combined deduction, she will receive income from a maximum amount of property. Furthermore, the entire amount of the marital deduction property is available to protect her against unforeseen needs.

Federal Income Tax Advantages

In addition to the federal estate tax advantages of charitable remainder trusts created under a will, there are also important federal income tax benefits. Generally speaking, the trustee pays no income tax on trust income, and where the principal goes to a charity no capital gains tax is payable by the trust on the sale of securities or other property held in the trust. This means that the trustee can invest and reinvest freely in the light of current market conditions, and the maximum possible amount of capital will always be available to earn income. Furthermore, because of recent changes in the law, creation of such a trust may also mean that the income beneficiary will not pay a tax at full ordinary income rates on all dollars received.

Maryland Income, Inheritance and Estate Taxes

The tax benefits of charitable remainder bequests under Maryland law are quite similar to those available under the federal law. With certain adjustments, the Maryland income and estate taxes are computed on the basis of figures supplied to the federal government. In addition, there is an exemption under the Maryland inheritance tax law for bequests to qualified Maryland charities and to charities in states which allow an exemption for bequests made by residents of their state to a Maryland charity.

Contingent Gifts Under a Will

Obviously, when a will is prepared, it is impossible to foresee the order of death or to be sure that beneficiaries will live to receive the property that is intended for them. Consequently, unless a final contingent beneficiary is named, property may ultimately pass to persons in whom the individual had little or no interest or, even worse, to the state.

The possibility that the ultimate beneficiaries will not live until the time of distribution is a contingency that should be dealt with in every estate plan. Very often, when considering this possibility, the property owner decides that a charitable organization should be named as the ultimate contingent beneficiary. Of course, where a trust is not involved, no charitable deduction is allowed unless the bequest is actually paid to charity at the death of the testator. However, where a bequest is so paid, the unlimited federal estate tax charitable deduction is available, the Maryland inheritance tax is avoided and no Maryland estate tax is paid on such a bequest.

Outright Gifts Made During Life

While gifts under wills have an obvious and direct effect on the probate estate, gifts made during life frequently have a vital indirect effect on probate planning. Outright gifts made during life often provide significant income tax deductions for the donor while also avoiding federal estate tax and Maryland death taxes on the value of the property comprising the gift. From a probate planning point of view, an outright gift to charity during life frequently has much the same effect as an outright bequest to charity, except of course that by reducing the size of the probate estate the lifetime gift may also produce a saving in the cost of settling the estate.

Charitable Remainder Gifts During Life

A great many people would like to make a substantial charitable gift during life, but feel they cannot afford a large outright gift of capital because of the future income that would be lost. For such persons, a charitable remainder gift made during life often proves attractive. It allows them to make a gift to charity while reserving income from the property for themselves and perhaps others as well. At the same time, the gift usually generates an income tax deduction, avoids capital gain taxes, reduces probate costs and provides federal estate tax and Maryland death tax savings.

Over the years, many charitable remainder gifts have been made during a donor's lifetime through the use of a charitable remainder trust. Under present law, if the value of a remainder interest given to charity in this way is to qualify for a federal income tax deduction, the trust must be either a charitable remainder *annuity trust* or *unitrust,* discussed earlier in this chapter.

As with outright gifts to charity, once a qualified charitable remainder gift is completed during life, the value of the gift property is excluded from the donor's estate for federal estate tax purposes and no Maryland inheritance tax or estate tax is payable. No capital gain tax is paid when property that has appreciated in value is placed in a qualified charitable remainder trust during life, and probate costs are avoided because the value of the trust property is not included in the donor-decedent's probate estate.

Gifts of Life Insurance

Life insurance has long been a popular means of making gifts to charity. Very often, the primary advantage of such a gift is that it enables the donor to make a much larger gift than he or she would otherwise have been able to make. For instance, a donor with adequate income but extensive commitments and little capital may not be able to leave a substantial charitable gift under his will. For such a person, life insurance is a means of providing a sizable capital gift through a comparatively small annual outlay, usually out of income.

Where the ownership of an existing policy is given during life to charity, the donor is usually entitled to an income tax deduction at the time of the gift. In addition, where a charitable organization owns an insurance policy, future premiums paid by the donor qualify for an income tax charitable deduction. On the other hand, if the donor owns any of the incidents of ownership of the policy, premium payments are not deductible. Consequently, no deductions are allowed for premiums paid on a policy which the insured continues to own, even though a charity is named as the beneficiary.

Where the ownership of a policy of insurance on the donor's life is given to charity during the insured's lifetime, the proceeds will not be subject to federal estate tax in his estate. However, if an individual retains ownership of a policy on his life until the date of his death, the proceeds will be included in his estate for federal estate tax purposes. But if the proceeds are paid to charity, a deduction is allowed in computing the amount of the estate tax. From a federal estate tax point of view, therefore, the insurance escapes the estate tax when the insured dies whether (1) the ownership of the policy is given to charity during life or (2) the proceeds are paid to charity at death. The insurance will also escape Maryland inheritance and estate taxes in either case. It must be remembered that a gift of the ownership of a life insurance policy means more than merely designating someone as the beneficiary of the policy; it means giving away to the donee the right to designate the beneficiary, the right to borrow against the policy and the right to surrender the policy for its cash value. See Chapter 14 for a more detailed discussion of life insurance.

Charitable Foundations

Many corporations and individuals of substantial means have created charitable trusts or corporations where both the income and principal are intended exclusively for charitable use. Such entities—sometimes called *foundations*—may exist permanently or for a limited period. They may be designed to achieve a single charitable objective or a number of such goals.

Where a foundation by reason of its operations or the pattern of its distributions is classified as a private foundation, the federal tax law (1) imposes a tax on its income, (2) severely limits the deduction for contributions to it and (3) imposes a host of other restrictions. There is not room in this chapter even to scratch the surface of recent changes in the ground rules applicable to private foundations. Suffice it to say that no such foundation should be created or operated today without guidance from an experienced attorney. Where property is given to a qualified foundation during life, the effect for probate planning purposes is much the same as though an outright gift to charity had been made during life. Where a foundation is created under a will, the effect for probate planning purposes is much the same as an outright gift to charity under a will.

8

Should I Make a Will?

While the question "Should I make a will?," is not as fundamental as the deeper inquiries of "Who am I?," "What am I doing here?" or "Where am I going?," it is a matter of concern to almost every intelligent person who, realizing he is the owner of property often accumulated through years of struggle, faces up to the discouraging fact that he is not immortal and wonders with ever-growing discomfort what he should do about it.

There are some who, unfortunately, fail to seek any answer to the question until it is too late. Others delay the moment of truth, usually (although often mistakenly) consoled either by their low estimate of the importance of their assets or by their faith that joint ownership of their assets with spouses, parents or children is a complete solution. Or they may rely blindly on the laws of intestacy and hope they will provide a satisfactory solution.

For the overwhelming majority of us the right answer to the question, "Should I make a will?," is a resounding, "Yes, by all means—and please let's do something about it right now!"

Everyone who has spent a considerable amount of energy to earn, save and conserve assets during years of effort and often at personal sacrifice will find it worthwhile to take the comparatively small amount of additional time and energy and pay the relatively small fee required to seek advice and come to an informed decision as to what should become of his property and possessions at his death.

A study of the property owned, the form in which it is held and the legal consequences of that form, as well as an up-to-date valuation of the property is often both revealing and surprising. For example, most of us tend to overlook the effect on our estates of the ever-increasing life insurance coverages in this era of group policies. These funds are often not used during one's life and tend to be forgotten in considering what will be available to our beneficiaries upon death.

For varied reasons many of us spend a lifetime trying to cram all of our property into the form of joint ownership with others, be it spouse, parent or children. In spite of these efforts, some individual assets usually escape joint holding, so that the question of the advisability of a will is still present. As a matter of fact, joint ownership itself cannot solve, and may often complicate, the whole problem. For example, a husband and a wife may hold all property in joint form and consider that neither needs a will. This may be true of the first one to die but certainly not of the second. A common disaster, like an unfortunate family auto tragedy, may remove the opportunity of executing a will, and intestacy is the inevitable result. Then, too, there are many important disadvantages to joint ownership, as will be emphasized in Chapter 12.

Leaving the whole matter of after-death distribution of assets to the intestacy laws is really a game of Russian roulette, for it is rare indeed that the statutory law will coincide exactly with anyone's personal wishes regarding the disposition of his property, both as to the identity of the recipients and the proportions or amounts each is to receive.

What Is a Will?

Simply stated, a will is a written document by which a person provides for the disposition of his property, to become effective on the date of his death. It is important to note that a will speaks only at the time of the testator's death. A maker of a will can change it as often as he wishes during his lifetime, in whole or in part. It conveys no property or rights until the maker dies, and therefore a will is capable of disposing of property and rights acquired before and after the will is made.

Who Can Make a Will?

Under present Maryland law any person may make a will if he or she is 18 years of age or older and legally competent.

The Execution of a Will

With the exceptions later noted, a will must be in writing, signed by the person making it (the testator), or by some other person for him, in his presence and by his express direction. In addition, the will must be witnessed by two or more credible persons who must sign their names in the presence of the testator. If such a witness does not see the testator actually sign the will, the testator must acknowledge, in the presence of the witness, that the document bearing his signature is his will.

Two exceptions are permitted to these rigid requirements: (1) a will which is entirely in the handwriting of a testator who is serving in the armed services is valid if signed by him, even though without witnesses, and (2) a written will not executed in Maryland is valid if signed by the testator and executed in conformity with the law of the testator's place of domicile or the place where the will is executed.

To make certain that all of the prerequisites for validity and the required formalities of execution are fully complied with, it is clearly advisable to have a competent attorney draw and supervise the execution of a will.

Who Receives Your Probate Estate if You Die without a Will?

Under the present Maryland statutes:

A. If your spouse survives you, he or she will receive:

1. If there is also surviving issue (meaning children or other descendants), one-third. (The children or descendants get the other two-thirds.)

2. If there is no surviving issue but a surviving parent, one-half. (The parent gets the other one-half.)

3. If there is no surviving issue or parent but a surviving brother or sister, or issue of a brother or sister, $4,000 plus one-half of the residue. (The rest goes to the brothers and sisters or their issue.)

4. If there is no surviving issue, parent, brother, sister or issue of a brother or sister, the whole.

B. If there is no surviving spouse, distribution will be made in the following order of priority:

1. Issue, in equal shares, by representation; or

2. Parents, equally if both survive, or entirely to a sole surviving parent; or

3. Brothers and sisters and their issue, in equal shares, by representation; or

4. To all surviving collateral relations in equal degree, without representation (but not beyond the tenth degree); or

5. Grandparents, equally if both survive, or entirely to a sole surviving grandparent.

C. If there is no person entitled to inheritance, as described above, the net probate estate will be converted to cash and paid to the board of education in the county where the estate is administered.

How many fathers with a modest or moderate estate, a wife and one young child would want his wife to receive at his death only one-third of his estate and the child two-thirds? The wife would likely have immediate personal financial problems in her efforts to support herself, while a guardianship under court supervision would normally be required for the child. And the inheritance of the child would not be readily available for the necessities of his mother.

Rarely would a husband without children prefer that only $4,000 plus a half of the rest of his net estate pass to his wife and the other half to his father or mother, or if they are deceased, to his brother or sister.

Yet, unless such a father or husband in these two examples executes a will, the statutory provisions will prevail and this kind of distribution is inevitable. Obviously, many other examples can be imagined where the failure to make a will leads to distribution according to the intestacy statutes, which would probably not conform to the decedent's wishes had he but made them known in a properly drawn and executed will.

Other Reasons for Making a Will

Let us consider, briefly, some of the more compelling reasons why each one of us—man or woman—should have a will that is up to date, one that takes into account the ever-changing conditions of human existence: marriage, divorce, parenthood, grandparenthood, the respective requirements, abilities and disabilities of beneficiaries, increase or decrease in assets and liabilities, deaths, the lack of constancy of one's desires and affections, as well as the continually changing tax laws and regulations.

1. The opportunity to name the personal representative who will administer your estate. It is important that you know what your personal representative will be called on to do and the competence required to fulfill these obligations. With this knowledge you can best make the decision as to who should be designated to serve. If you die without a will, someone else will necessarily make that important determination.

2. The creation of trusts for the protection of your estate and the welfare of your beneficiaries. If you do not create a living trust during your lifetime, only by will can you arrange for the many advantages that a trust or trusts may make possible over a period of many years for the benefit of those you care for. For example, the financial care of minor children and of aged or disabled relatives, with sufficient discretion given to the trustee and with flexibility permitting modifications which can be accomplished by a trust, provide tremendous reassurance and comfort to the man or woman who executes a will.

3. The nomination of the guardian for the personal care of your minor children, if your spouse too has died. The guardian should be the person who, in your opinion, would most closely take your place as a parent.

4. The excusing of debts or the payment of outstanding mortgages.

5. The avoidance of undesired disposition of your assets by virtue of an unfortunate common disaster.

6. Tax savings, without impairment of fundamental wishes as to who should receive the benefit of your estate.

Summary

Each responsible and thoughtful person who has property, real or personal, owes a primary obligation to those dependent on him or her to take the time to consider carefully the financial impact of his or her death. In addition, he or she alone should have the opportunity to decide who shall be beneficiaries of the estate, in what proportions, under what circumstances the property is to be given, and by whom it is to be held, invested, administered and distributed. A carefully and properly prepared will containing the necessary provisions to carry out the desires of the testator is the answer to such obligation and opportunity.

9

What Should My Will Contain?

A well-drawn will is tailored to the individual desires, needs and circumstances of the person who signs it, the testator. An ideal provision in the will of one person might be unfit, and even dangerous, if used in the will of another. Nevertheless, there are numerous provisions that are included in most wills, and there are various problems that should be considered in the drawing of any will.

A will should set forth the place of residence of the person who signs it and should contain a statement that all prior wills of that person are revoked.

If the testator has any particular desires about the disposition of his remains, these should be stated. If he wishes to donate his body or any parts (for example, his eyes to the Eye Bank) for medical purposes and has not otherwise made such provisions, he may do so in his will. Of course, it is important also to communicate these desires to the family, and to the hospital or agency concerned, because speed is important and wills are often not read until after the funeral.

Appointment of a Personal Representative

A personal representative is a person (or more than one person), a bank, or a combination of both. The personal representative, after the death of a testator, carries out the instructions in the will, pays the debts, prepares the inventories, accounts and tax returns, sees that the taxes are paid, and protects and manages the property until it can be delivered to the beneficiaries. Until the Maryland probate law was changed recently, a personal representative named by will was called an executor. If a will does not appoint a personal representative, the probate court, known as the Orphans' Court in most Maryland jurisdictions, will select someone. To avoid possible confusion and delay and to insure that the property will be handled by someone in whom the testator has trust and confidence, the testator should appoint a personal representative in his will. It is also desirable that the will name an alternate personal representative in case the person first named is unable or unwilling to serve.

Unless the will excuses an individual personal representative from giving bond or all persons interested in the estate waive it, the probate court will require that the person named as personal representative furnish a bond, usually equal to the value of the personal estate, to guarantee the faithful performance of his duties. If the will excuses the bond, then only a nominal bond equal to the debts and Maryland taxes need be furnished. The cost of the bond will be paid out of the testator's estate. Consequently, a testator should decide whether he desires to minimize this cost by specifying in the will that only a nominal bond need be given.

Provision for Payment of Debts and Taxes

Even though a will does not contain instructions to pay debts and taxes of the testator, a personal representative has a general duty to do so. Nevertheless, wills ordinarily contain such instructions, and there is value in this since the testator can spell out his exact wishes about debts and taxes. If, for example, the testator is making installment mortgage payments on his home, does he wish to have his estate pay off the mortgage in full upon his death, or does he want the personal representative, and thereafter his widow or some other beneficiary, to continue the installment payments? If continuing the installment payments is desired, the will should say so.

Regarding tax payments, does the testator intend that certain property or bequests shall be inherited tax free with the taxes being paid out of other assets in the estate, or does he want the person receiving the property to pay the proportionate amounts of inheritance or estate tax on it? A will should answer this question, rather than leaving it to an interpretation of the law or for the personal representative.

Provisions Disposing of the Property

The principal provisions in most wills are those which set forth to whom and in what manner the testator's property shall pass upon his death. In Maryland, a spouse is entitled to receive a portion of the estate and may decide to receive that portion regardless of the provisions made for her in the will. This portion is referred to as a statutory share of the estate and replaces the old provision for dower, which no longer exists in Maryland. Except for this requirement about the spouse, a testator may leave his property to anyone—relative or not—for a good reason, a bad reason, or no reason at all; and he may "disinherit" the rest of the family.

Likewise, a testator has great freedom of choice in determining how his property shall go to the person named in his will. He can give the property outright; he can put the property in a trust; or he can give the property on condition that the person receiving it do, or refrain from doing, whatever the testator specifies. Similarly, he can provide that the person receiving the property is to enjoy it only during his lifetime (or for a certain period of time), and that thereafter the property will go to another.

There are certain technical restrictions on a testator's power to leave his property in his will. For example, he must not try to control the property for too long, and he must not direct that it be used for an unlawful purpose or for a purpose that violates so-called "public policy." However, subject only to such restrictions, a testator can and should have his will written so that his property will be disposed of in the exact manner he desires. The aim of the lawyer who writes the will should be to find out what the testator wants to do with his property and then, keeping in mind tax consequences, to word the will so that it carries out those desires as fully as possible.

Since a testator has such wide latitude in determining how the provisions of his will are to be written, only a few general comments need to be made about them. First and foremost, the will should be written so that it covers all of the testator's property. If this is not done, costly court proceedings may be necessary regarding the omitted property. To guard against an omission, a will should always contain a catch-all provision that all property of every kind that has not been disposed of by other portions of the will shall go in a specified manner.

If a testator is putting his property into a trust or is otherwise tying up its future use and enjoyment, he should be sure to consider whether he wants his home, its furnishings, his automobile and his personal effects to be included with the other property in the trust or whether he wants his widow or other beneficiary to have the free and unrestricted ownership of those properties. Tangible personal assets which are consumed or worn out by use seldom belong in a trust.

Many wills contain specific bequests directing that specific pieces of property or sums of money shall go to certain persons, followed by a general bequest in which the rest of the property is left to others. Thus, a testator may give a shotgun to a friend, a sum of money to a faithful employee, a farm to a certain relative and so on, with those portions of the will being followed by a general provision giving the rest of his property to his widow, or to her and to his children.

Usually, the persons who are to receive the rest of the property are those whom the testator is most interested in benefiting. A change in circumstances from the time a will is signed to the time the testator dies can be a danger to these persons in a will of this type and, as a result, the will may deny benefits to the very persons he wished most to benefit. For example, say a widower had property worth $100,000 in 1966 when he signed his will. He wanted his children to receive the biggest part of his estate, so he worded his will so that five friends or other relatives each receive $5,000, with the rest of the estate going to his children. However, if his estate has shrunk to $25,000 by the time he dies, the $5,000 bequests will use up the entire estate and, even though the testator intended that his children would receive most of his property, they will get nothing.

Consequently, whenever a testator is thinking about making specific bequests and then leaving the bulk of his estate to those dearest to him, he should bear in mind the effect of a decline in the value of the estate. A possible solution is to make the specific bequests in terms of fractional parts of the estate rather than in terms of dollars. Thus, in the example cited the testator with an original estate of $100,000 should have made the five specific bequests by giving each person 1/20th of his estate, instead of giving $5,000 to each. Then, when the estate had shrunk to $25,000 the five specific bequests would require only $6,250 of the estate, leaving $18,750 for the children.

Provision for Alternate Disposition of Property

When a testator provides in his will that most of his property shall go to a certain person, ordinarily it is wise for him also to provide for a secondary beneficiary in the event that the first person dies before the will takes effect. A chain of alternatives is ordinarily unnecessary and may lead to legal problems, but at least one alternate disposition of the property is customary and wise.

Provision for Death from a Common Accident

It is not unusual for a husband and wife to be killed as a result of a common accident or under circumstances which make it impossible to determine who died first. Since the husband's will usually provides for the wife to take some or all of his property, and vice versa, this type of accident may create problems.

Maryland has a statute to cover simultaneous deaths which declares that the testator is presumed to have survived the beneficiary. In such an event, the estate will be distributed as if the beneficiary had predeceased the testator. Maryland also has a statute which requires, unless the will provides otherwise, that all beneficiaries of a will except a spouse must survive the testator by 30 days in order to receive a bequest. In many cases, these statutes will cover the situation and no contrary provisions need be stated in the will. Often, however, a testator may wish to avail his estate of the marital deduction for federal estate tax purposes by declaring in his will that in the event of simultaneous deaths, his wife will be presumed to have survived him.

Taxes are not always the controlling factor, however. Suppose a husband's will leaves all his property to his wife with an alternate gift to his family in the event that she dies before he does, and the wife has left all her property to the husband with an alternate gift to her family. Then, in a common accident the husband dies first and the wife dies 10 minutes later. Immediately upon the husband's death, title to his property will go to his wife; and then minutes later, when the wife dies, title to the property will go to her family eliminating his family entirely. Depending on their desires, the husband's will could have contained a clause requiring his wife to survive him by a stated number of days.

Powers for the Personal Representative

The will should give the personal representative broad powers to settle the estate and special wording should be used to provide these powers. Although Maryland law now gives a personal representative many powers in the performance of his duties, well-defined powers in a will include areas not covered by the law.

Provision for Guardianship

When the testator has minor children, the will should always appoint a guardian to serve in the event that he is the surviving parent and dies before his children have attained their majority. After his 16th birthday, a child may select a guardian of his property subject to court approval. For the guidance of the court, however, it is still wise to name a guardian in the will, even though the children are over 16.

Required Formalities

A will executed in Maryland must be in writing, signed by the testator or by some other person for him, in his presence and by his express direction and declared by the testator to be his will to at least two witnesses who must also sign the will in the presence of the testator. Normally, a clause reciting these facts follows the signature of the testator after which the witnesses sign.

Summary

In Maryland, except for the statutory share to which the spouse is entitled, a testator has an almost unlimited freedom in determining to whom and how his property shall pass upon his death. His will should be tailor-made to carry out his wishes and meet the individual needs and circumstances of his estate. However, unless certain formalities are observed and certain common problems are considered, the desires of the testator may be frustrated; the beneficiaries named in his will may get nothing or may receive an estate greatly decreased by unnecessary and costly administrative expenses, death taxes, income taxes and litigation. In addition to containing carefully drawn provisions disposing of the testator's property, a will should, at the very least, name a personal representative and give him ample powers to preserve and settle the estate.

10

Pitfalls in a Homemade Will

Ye lawyers who live upon litigants' fees,
And who need a good many to live at your ease,
* * *
When a festive occasion your spirit unbends,
You should never forget the Profession's best friends;
So we'll send round the wine and bright bumper fill,
To the jolly testator who makes his own will.

Lord Neaves

A testator who decides to make his own will no doubt thinks he is saving money by avoiding the payment of a legal fee. If so, he is likely to be making one of the costliest mistakes of his life.

Preparing an effective estate plan and drawing a good will are like navigating difficult waters. It is work for an expert. Unlike the layman, the lawyer has been trained to avoid the obstacles and use the instruments that will achieve safe harbor.

The law books are full of reports of lengthy and expensive trials and appeals that were necessary because laymen-amateurs tried to save a few dollars by a do-it-yourself approach to estate planning and will drafting.

The subject of wills fills many pages in large and highly technical learned legal treatises. Every legal point in every such treatise can be a pitfall. A complete discussion of the pitfalls of will drafting would require a book many times the size of this one. All that can be done here is to convey a general idea of the major types of reefs upon which wills drawn by laymen may founder.

There are three major types of difficulty with homemade wills: (1) the will is not properly executed; (2) the language of the will is not clear because the draftsman has failed to be aware of problems which a lawyer would have foreseen, or simply because the draftsman lacks sufficient skill in the use of precise English; and (3) the lay draftsman is unaware of the horrible complications of tax laws and other legal rules, as well as practical considerations relating to estates, which can impair and even thwart the accomplishment of the testator's goals.

Proper Execution of the Will

One of the dangers of a will written without professional advice is that the maker may not give sufficient attention to the legal requirements for the execution of a will. If these requirements are not followed, the writing cannot be admitted to probate as a will. Thousands of "wills," including many which were entirely in the handwriting of the testator, have been denied probate in Maryland. They have been completely ineffective because they were not executed in the manner required by law.

In addition to the protection a lawyer will provide against the possibility that a will may be ineffective because not properly executed, there is another good reason for having a lawyer supervise the execution of a will. The lawyer provides witnesses who will be available for testimony at a later date if they are needed. He will advise the best way to safeguard the original document, and he will complete a copy and retain it in his files to evidence the contents of the original. Such evidence may be important if the original becomes lost or inadvertently destroyed.

The Unclear Will

Here are some typical examples of language in wills drawn by laymen, which may at first glance seem perfectly clear and nontechnical. The use of such provisions has resulted in serious problems because the language, though seemingly clear, is actually imprecise, or the testator has failed to think his problem through fully.

1. *Everything to the wife—what's left to the children.* An expression which is sometimes found in a will written without legal advice is, "I give my wife everything I have, and upon her death I give what is left for the benefit of my children." Problems are created by such phrasing. Does the wife get the property, or only the right to use it for life? May she sell, mortgage or lease the property, and if so, how may she invest the proceeds of sale? What happens if the wife mingles the husband's property with her own (including what she may acquire after his death)? Can she give the property away during her lifetime? The words "for the benefit of" may create a trust. Is a trust created for the children? If a trust is created, who is the trustee and what are the terms of the trust? When does the trust come to an end? These are merely some of the questions raised by such wording, and the answers come only after costly legal proceedings—much more expensive than if the testator had paid a fee to have his will drawn properly.

2. *Gift of money.* If a testator states, "I give $25,000 to my three sons," does he mean $25,000 to be divided among

the three sons, or does he mean $25,000 to each?

3. *Gift of land.* If testator declares, "I give all my land in Baltimore County to my son," and the land is subject to a mortgage, does testator mean that the son should have to pay the mortgage, or that the mortgage should be paid by the estate?

4. *Money on deposit in a bank.* Another type of ambiguity is that involved in a gift of money on deposit in a bank. Does the statement, "I leave to my son, John, the money on deposit at the First National Bank," mean only what was on hand when the will was made, say $1,000, or when the decedent died, say $25,000? And, if it turns out that at his death there are two bank accounts, namely, a checking account he had when he made his will and a savings account he opened later, who gets what?

5. *Gifts of shares of stock.* A recurring problem is the gift of a specific number of shares of stock without reference to stock splits or stock dividends. For example, the testator may give 100 shares of XYZ stock. When the testator dies, he owns 105 shares because after he signed his will there was a 5% stock dividend. Has the testator thought about this problem, and what is his intention as to how many shares the legatee should really have?

6. *Gift of a business interest.* Consider the following statement: "I give my business to my son." Does testator mean "business" to include the accounts receivable, the inventories, the cash in the bank and other assets belonging to the business? How about the accounts payable? What if the business is located on a piece of land owned by the testator; who is intended to get the land?

7. *Expression of "desire" or "request".* Sometimes a testator leaves property to a relative or friend and makes a "request" or expresses a "desire" that the legatee use the property in a certain way or for certain purposes. Often it has required a court case to decide whether this kind of language requires the legatee to act in accordance with the testator's

request or desire, or whether the legatee can decide to reject the testator's request or desire and still keep the legacy.

8. *The problem of unanticipated death.* One of the frequent sources of lack of clarity in wills is the problem of unanticipated death. If a legatee named in the will dies before the testator, does the testator intend the bequest to lapse or should the wife or children of the legatee take the legacy or some part of it? This question is particularly important where a testator leaves his estate to his "children equally" and one child dies before the testator, leaving children who survive the testator. Does the testator want his children who survive him to take everything or does he also want to provide for the children of the child who predeceased him? Is a gift to "my wife for life and upon her death to my surviving children" intended to include a child who survives the testator but does not survive the wife, or is it intended to cut out such a child even if that child leaves children surviving both father and mother?

The Faulty Will

The following are examples of provisions of wills which may be perfectly clear, but which fail to attain the testator's goal because they do not take account of tax law or various important legal doctrines and practical considerations of which a layman is not likely to be aware.

1. *More taxes than necessary.* Federal and state death tax laws are very complicated. Drawing a proper will requires adequate knowledge of these laws which a layman ordinarily does not have. Professor W. Barton Leach of the Harvard Law School has pointed out that President Coolidge's will probably caused his family to pay almost twice as much in federal death taxes as actually should have been paid. President Coolidge's will said with characteristic brevity: "Not unmindful of my son, John, I give all my estate, both real and personal, to my wife, Grace Coolidge, in fee simple." This

provision seems perfectly clear. However, at the time President Coolidge died it meant a tax on all the property in his estate and another tax on everything that remained in Mrs. Coolidge's estate when she died. Professor Leach pointed out to the law students for whom his casebook was written that the proper drafting of a power of appointment (something not likely to be within the knowledge or skill of a layman) would have enabled the property to go at Mrs. Coolidge's death to John, to whom the President and Mrs. Coolidge would probably have wanted it to go, while at the same time giving Mrs. Coolidge full protection and avoiding any tax in her estate. The specific tax laws have changed since President Coolidge's death, but the principle of the illustration is still fully valid.

2. *The futile will.* Not all property in which a testator has some interest can be left by will. Property in joint names, pension benefits and life insurance proceeds are examples of property which a will may not be able to affect. If all the testator's property consists of such assets, any will he draws may be simply futile. In that case, a will must be supplemented by necessary changes in the way such property is held during the testator's lifetime. In any event, in order to have a sensible and effective estate plan, the provisions of the will must be integrated with deeds, bank book titles, insurance and other contracts of the testator, so that all of his property will go at his death, whether under the will or otherwise, in accordance with his overall plan.

3. *The incomplete will.* Many important matters are often overlooked in the self-made will. There may be a failure to give directions to an executor as to what to do about taxes due on a life insurance policy. The estate without the insurance may be quite small, but the large insurance policy will cause the estate to have to pay an estate tax. Who should pay the tax on the insurance proceeds—the individual named in the policy or the persons entitled to the residue of the estate under the will?

The self-made will may fail to designate an alternate personal representative or trustee in the event the originally named personal representative or trustee fails or ceases to serve. In the absence of the designation of a successor, the administration would have to proceed with a personal representative appointed by the court.

Sufficient attention may not be given to the possibility of one death occurring within a short time of another. If a testator gives all his property to a surviving wife, all the property may go to her family to the complete exclusion of his family, even though there may be only a few minutes difference in the times of their deaths.

Other important problems a lay testator often fails to think about and properly provide for include: a spendthrift clause to protect against creditors of a beneficiary; a trust or trusts to provide necessary protection and flexibility; on what basis to choose a personal representative or trustee; the desirability of postponing complete and outright distribution to children beyond the age of 21; minimizing the disturbance of the testator's estate plan which can occur if a surviving spouse renounces her rights under the will and takes the snare which the law gives her; the selection of a guardian for minor children; and whether legacies of money should have the inheritance taxes paid out of the estate instead of having the legatee pay such taxes out of the legacy, as is normally required in the absence of a special provision in the will.

4. *The distorted will.* If a testator prepares his own will, he may produce consequences he really does not want, as well as fail to accomplish what he does want. For example, a testator writing his own will sometimes makes large bequests of money to friends or certain relatives, and leaves the rest or residue of his estate to his wife and children, who are the primary objects of his bounty. As a result of unanticipated change in circumstances, his estate when he dies may be much smaller than he thought it would be when he made the

will. After payment of the money bequests, there may be little or nothing left for his wife and children.

5. *The invalid bequest.* There are certain legal limitations on the power to dispose of property by will. For example, there are complicated limits set by the rule against perpetuities on how long the vesting of interests left in trust may be postponed, and there are certain conditions testators have tried to impose on their legatees, such as illegal restraints on alienation and various other conditions against public policy, which the law will strike down. Only a lawyer can advise whether the law permits particular objectives to be carried out and if it does not, then suggest the closest permissible alternative.

Summary

The examples given above are only a few reasons why it is not advisable for a person inexperienced in legal terms and consequences to attempt to draw his own will. Homemade wills are a prolific source of family disputes and cause litigation, bitterness and greatly increased costs of probate.

While the "jolly testator who makes his own will" may in a certain sense be humorously called the legal profession's "best friend," it is hoped that such best friends will become fewer and fewer and eventually disappear. The real best friends of the legal profession are those who have been competently assisted in steering clear of the pitfalls that produce expensive, wasteful and unnecessary litigation.

11

Who Should
Settle Your Estate?

Name the Right Personal Representative

Choosing the proper personal representative (frequently called "executor") is one of the most vital decisions a testator must face in planning a will. The one appointed will be the testator's agent to carry out the wishes and desires expressed in the will. The decision has an important bearing on (1) the skillfulness with which the estate will be settled, (2) the savings that will be achieved, and (3) the benefits (which he has worked so hard to accumulate) that will pass to the objects of his bounty. Important elements to consider in a personal representative are integrity, business experience, impartiality, availability to serve and sound judgment.

Duties and Powers

The personal representative is not a figurehead, and the position should never be viewed merely as a mark of distinction or honor. The ultimate goal is to handle the estate in the very best interests of the beneficiaries who will inherit it. The personal representative has the responsibility of winding up the testator's financial affairs and conserving the assets in the estate through careful management. The personal representative accordingly must become deeply involved in the decedent's financial and business problems; in the solution of these problems the personal representative's judgment is substituted for the testator's. The treatment of the estate's assets should be fair, impartial and confidential.

The powers conferred upon a personal representative in a will should be broad enough to include the operation of a business, the manner of disposing of property and, finally, of making division among the legatees. Estate administration by the personal representative may, depending on the circumstances, continue for several years, or it may be completed in a short time.

The personal representative, in the performance of his duties, may exercise any power or authority conferred upon him in the will, without application to or approval of the court. Except as limited by the will or by an order of court, a personal representative may, in addition to any power or authority contained in the will, properly exercise broad general powers provided by statute.

In any estate where a personal representative is named in the will, certain procedures are required. Following the testator's death, the will should be taken immediately to the attorney representing the estate, who will file an application for its probate. The personal representative should know generally the nature and extent of the decedent's properties. After application is made by petition, administrative probate is granted by the Register of Wills and the will is admitted to probate and record. Notice must be published and circulated to "interested persons" (legatees and closest relatives). Any interested person may, within four months, insist on judicial probate, in which case certain procedures are thereafter required to be followed in the Orphans' Court.

If no judicial probate is requested, the personal representative who has qualified before the Register has the authority to act in administering the estate. He is responsible for locating and managing the properties left by the testator and must determine the debts owed by the decedent. He must prepare a list of the properties to be included in an inventory, some of which must be appraised by qualified appraisers. Should there be a going business, he must supervise it. It is most important that the properties be properly insured and the necessary policy endorsements obtained.

The personal representative is required to give all notices required to interested parties, prepare all necessary tax returns and pay all taxes. After payment of allowable debts and expenses of his administration, he prepares such accounts as may be required and makes distribution to the legatees as directed under the will.

Who, then, should be chosen as the personal representative?

The Surviving Spouse

The surviving spouse may be capable of assuming the responsibilities of administering the estate. Frequently, however, a widow (or even a widower) is untrained in the handling of probate and tax problems involved in the estate. In such instances it may be advisable for a testator to name his lawyer as personal representative, or he may want to name a bank, a partner, another family member, or a trusted friend. Eventually, the surviving spouse may be required to manage her own affairs but this can come gradually as she acquires some knowledge of the problems involved. The widow always could and many times should serve as a co-personal representative with the lawyer or other personal representative. In the capacity of co-personal representative, the surviving spouse can act together with the steadying hand of one more experienced in probate matters.

A Bank

Many banks have been granted fiduciary powers. Their trust departments are supervised by state and federal authorities. As personal representative, a bank retains an attorney—almost always the attorney who drew the will—to advise it in handling the estate. Even if a bank is not named as personal representative, there are instances in larger estates where a bank is employed by the personal representative to act as custodian for securities and to collect and keep records of dividends and interest and to perform other transactions.

Fees

The personal representative will be entitled to compensation allowable by law in Maryland. The law (Section 7-601 of Article 93 of the Annotated Code) provides a personal representative with reasonable compensation for his services. (See Chapter 21.) An individual, whether the surviving spouse, a child or a trusted friend, is entitled to request payment of an amount up to the full allowable commissions as personal representative but may, and frequently does, serve in such capacity, waiving all or a substantial part of the commissions. Where this happens the lawyer's fee becomes the only charge against the estate. (Chapter 21 discusses fully the costs of probate.)

A Substitute Personal Representative

The personal representative must, of course, live longer than the testator. It is advisable, therefore, to name one or more alternates, with the same powers and rights as the first personal representative. If a bank is named, there is of course no question of the permanence of the appointment.

Co-Personal Representatives

As indicated above, the testator may consider appointing two or more personal representatives. This arrangement often removes the fear of possible friction in the family when one child is named over another. However, consideration should be given as to whether there is danger of disputes between co-personal representatives. And possible conflicts of interest among various candidates should not be overlooked.

The personal representative cannot act until the will is admitted to probate and letters of administration are granted, whether by administrative or judicial probate. There may, however, be certain urgent matters requiring immediate attention before the personal representative can formally qualify. Should the testator be engaged in a going business or have perishable assets in the estate, continued operation and protection will be required. It may be necessary to arrange for funds to subsidize the operation of a going business. Therefore, in choosing personal representatives, consideration should be given to the appointment of persons or institutions (or both) who have the willingness, ability and flexibility to take over promptly and act with competence to settle the decedent's estate.

Telling Your Personal Representative

An individual personal representative should generally be consulted before being named in a will to determine whether he is willing to act. Following the preparation of the will, it is a good practice to furnish the personal representative with a copy or to advise him of the location of the original will. Frequently, originals of wills are left with the attorney, or with a bank if the bank is named as a personal representative.

It would be the unusual case when the testator did not advise the attorney preparing the will of the location of the original will. The notation on the interview record of the attorney often provides a source of information to the interested parties seeking its location.

Consider the case of a married couple having separate wills, each containing a provision for death in a common disaster and the handling of their estates by a personal representative and trustee for the benefit of minor children. Upon the occurrence of such a contingency, and if the wills are not readily available to the personal representatives, proceedings for administration of the estates might be delayed. An estate might even be administered by a person unaware that wills exist, with results different from those planned by the decedents. There have even been instances where an estate has been closed before the will was discovered.

Attributes of a Personal Representative

There is never a substitute for knowledge and experience, and considerations in appointing the personal representative are much the same as those given to choosing a business associate. The necessary attributes may be summarized as follows:

Integrity. The personal representative should have the ultimate interest of the beneficiaries in mind at all times. This requires soundness of moral principles and character. Unselfishness and honesty must be exercised in all dealings with the estate.

Business ability. Sound business judgment combined with experience is a desired quality. Many economies are gained from experience, resulting in fulfillment of the testator's ultimate desire of having as much of the estate as possible distributed to the beneficiaries named in the will.

Administrative ability. Handling an estate requires knowledge of the rights and responsibilities of a personal representative and the ability to carry them out. In handling most estates, even those of modest size, a knowledge of the law governing income taxation as well as estate and inheritance taxation is absolutely essential. Another important qualification that is easily stated but frequently has far-reaching ramifications is the ability and competence to evaluate the assets. This quality is especially important if the testator owns an interest in a closely held business.

Availability. Time is an important factor in handling the estate and depends on its size and complexity. If the personal representative is to keep the best interests of the beneficiaries in mind, he must have the time to devote to the administration of the estate. In large estates, the duties may be so time-consuming that some individuals named to serve as personal representatives would have to neglect their own business interests. In such cases, testators should consider appointing a competent attorney or a bank. It may be wise, in some cases, to have an individual, who may be a relative or an attorney, serve with a bank if one is appointed.

Impartiality. Whether the personal representative is the surviving spouse, child, friend, attorney, trust institution, or any combination of these, complete impartiality is required. Such impartiality may be impossible from a member of the family. For example, if there are several children and only one is working in the family business, which is the chief asset of the estate, impartiality may be difficult to achieve within the family. Should he believe this to be the case, the testator must go outside the family. Again, if a bank happens to be a substantial creditor of a closely held business, there could possibly be a serious conflict of interest if it also is a personal representative.

Discretion. Handling an estate may bring the personal representative into contact with family problems which neither the testator nor his survivors desire to have publicly aired. It is therefore important that the personal representatives conduct estate administration with complete discretion. It is the privilege of the personal representatives to serve the deceased, and it is the right of the testator to expect that matters held in confidence during his lifetime will be so maintained after his death.

Summary

The office of personal representative is an important privilege. A testator intends that the accumulations of a lifetime should be handled prudently. Consequently, he should select a personal representative who possesses training in tax law and probate procedures and sound business judgment, tempered with concern for the beneficiaries of the estate.

In recent years, people have given more thought and attention to planning their estates than in the past. This is attributable to the ever-growing difficulty in accumulating, managing, preserving and passing along property. Taxation and its adverse effects are of special concern. Any mistake in judgment or delay in action can be costly. An inexperienced personal representative or one who lacks knowledge of his duties can cause unnecessary losses or additional expenses. A will, no matter how simple, should be made for every property owner, and its preparation should include earnest attention to the selection of a personal representative. A personal representative, in order to serve the estate in the most beneficial manner must be capable, knowledgeable and experienced, always exercising seasoned judgment and devoting such time to the estate affairs as may be required to discharge the manifold and complex duties involved.

12

Will Substitutes— Jointly Owned Property

A Warning

Unfortunately, space here does not afford a full discussion of joint tenancy, which is a most important matter and also a most complicated one. The best advice which can be given to the reader is that he should not lightly register securities or set up bank accounts in joint names. He (and she) should first seek advice from the family lawyer or accountant before creating any joint tenancy ownership of property with a spouse or anyone else. A small checking or savings account in joint tenancy with one's spouse may be quite satisfactory. Beyond that, be warned: creating a joint tenancy without careful consideration can cause expensive tax results and place the ultimate ownership of the property in unexpected hands. Actually, if a law were passed in Maryland to void all joint tenancies created by persons without advice of an attorney or accountant, a great number of still-to-happen family disputes, litigation and expensive tax traps could be eliminated. There is more misinformation and bad advice given by non-lawyers concerning joint tenancies than perhaps any other subject in the law.

Origin

Many people believe that an ideal method of owning property is "joint tenancy with right of survivorship." The ownership of property with right of survivorship is not a new idea. It was an early common law favorite. If two persons bought property and had title taken in both names, the presumption was that they intended to own it with right of survivorship. So, if land was purchased by Cox and Box (not husband and wife), and if neither sold his interest prior to the death of one, the survivor owned the entire property interest. The reasoning was that when one died, his interest in the tract also died, and the survivor owned all. This was their agreement.

From a practical standpoint, the chief characteristic of joint tenancy is that the survivor owns the entire interest. The appealing aspect is the saving of time and expenses in probate by permitting the survivor to own the property automatically. In the early common law of England, the purpose of joint tenancy was to minimize or avoid feudal tenures and duties, the predecessors of present-day death taxes.

In time the chief characteristic lost its appeal, partly because of abolition of the early feudal taxes and partly because it became less desirable to have the ultimate ownership dependent on the gamble of survival. The owner of a joint interest could not dispose of it by his will. If he died without a will, his interest would not go to his heirs. If a joint tenant wanted his interest to go at his death to somebody other than his joint tenant, the joint tenancy had to be severed during the lives of the joint tenants. The presumption of feudal times changed during subsequent common law development from that favoring right of survivorship to that favoring a tenancy in common ownership. So then, if Cox and Box bought land together, it was presumed that they owned it as tenants in common. Unlike the joint tenancy earlier favored, if Cox died, his interest would pass under his will, and if he died without a will, his interest would go to his heirs; at his death the survivor would not own any more interest than he owned before the death of his co-tenant. The chief characteristic of co-tenancy, then, is that the deceased co-tenant's interest passes as a part of his estate. In the case of husband and wife, however, a special form of joint ownership is still favored. This is known as tenancy by the entireties; neither spouse, while alive, can dispose of his or her interest in the property without the consent of the other, but on death it passes to the survivor.

The Maryland rule today is that if two persons (not husband and wife) buy property as joint tenants with right of survivorship and not as tenants in common (or words of similar meaning showing this intent), the survivor owns the entire interest at the death of the other. It can be seen clearly by their express agreement that they intended that the survivor take all. But in the absence of this agreement, it is felt that the ultimate ownership of property should not be determined by chance of survival.

Many states have express statutes concerning these ancient presumptions. The majority of these statutes, including the one in Maryland, provide that if parties (other than husband and wife) buy property, it shall be presumed that they do not own it with right of survivorship. In most states the right of survivorship is possible, but it must be clearly shown by the language of the deed or other instrument of title that this was the intention of the owners. Where husband and wife buy property without any indication of the type of tenancy intended to be created, the presumption is that a tenancy by the entirety is created.

The simplicity of survivorship has always been appealing; this convenient and inexpensive method of passing ownership of property is available today under Maryland law. Although it is not a fair statement that property should never be held in survivorship form in order to save time, money and possible litigation at an owner's death, neither is it fair to say that all property should be held in survivorship form.

In the 1930s there arose one other reason for holding property owned by a husband in his name and his wife's. Bankruptcies were rampant, and property so held, unless transferred in fraud of creditors after an owner was in financial trouble, was (and still is) free from claims of creditors of the husband.

Types of Joint Ownership in Maryland and Methods of Creation

Today in Maryland there are a number of forms of joint ownership, including tenancy by the entireties, joint tenancy with right of survivorship and tenancy in common. A conveyance to a husband and wife creates a tenancy by the entireties unless there is indication that some other form of ownership is intended. A conveyance to two persons who are not husband and wife, if there are no words indicating that a joint tenancy with right of survivorship is intended, will result in a tenancy in common.

In Maryland, a tenancy by the entireties can exist only between husband and wife. Where property is held by the entireties, one spouse cannot sever or sell his or her interest without the consent of the other spouse. Upon the death of the first spouse to die, the property passes immediately to the survivor by operation of law; it does not pass under the will of the first spouse to die. Generally, creditors of either spouse alone cannot attach the property.

Where property is held in a joint tenancy with right of survivorship, each joint tenant can sever or sell his or her interest without the consent of the other party. The property would then be held as a tenancy in common. Creditors of one joint owner can generally attach such an interest. The property would then be held as a tenancy in common. Upon the death of the first of two joint tenants to die, the property passes immediately to the survivor by operation of law; it does not pass under the will of the first to die.

Either of two tenants in common can sever or sell his interest without the consent of the other party. Upon the death of a tenant in common, his or her interest passes by will or by the laws of intestate succession if there is not a will; the property does not pass to the surviving co-tenant.

Problems Associated with Joint Ownership

Before talking about the problems of joint ownership, it should be emphasized that many considerations recommend placing the residence of a husband and wife in joint ownership, arising from the very nature of marriage and of the family relationship. Lawyers usually feel that these considerations override in most instances the other legal objections set forth in the balance of this chapter. Consequently, homeowners should not feel that the argument against joint ownership necessarily applies to ownership of a family home.

A number of disadvantages can arise from an unconsidered use of joint ownership. First, the person who actually purchases the property may find it taxed upon the prior death of the other joint tenant. Let us take the example of Mr. Evans. He purchases an apartment house for investment and takes title with his wife as tenants by the entireties. Upon the death of Mrs. Evans (she dies first), the Internal Revenue Service will take the position that the house was owned by her, should be included in her estate, and should be subject to federal estate tax in her estate. Unless Mrs. Evans' personal representative is able to show by convincing evidence that Mr. Evans supplied the purchase price for the house, the value of the house would be included in Mrs. Evans' estate. It is often difficult, if not impossible, however, to show who actually supplied the funds used to purchase the jointly owned property. If the purchase price is paid from a joint account, for instance, a very involved task of tracing deposits and withdrawals will be necessary to show that Mr. Evans, rather than Mrs. Evans, paid for the apartment house.

Mr. Evans also purchased securities and placed them in his name and that of his nephew as joint tenants with the right of survivorship. Upon the unexpected death of the nephew, Mr. Evans was surprised and not at all pleased to find that he was liable for an inheritance tax at the rate of 7 1/2% on one-half of the value of the securities at the time of his nephew's death. (See also Chapter 5, which deals more fully with Maryland inheritance taxes.)

Joint ownership by husband and wife may have very unfortunate consequences which do not appear until the death of the survivor. The marital deduction, which is discussed in Chapter 6, permits approximately one-half of one spouse's estate to pass to the other spouse free of federal estate tax. But the marital deduction is limited to one-half of the deceased's adjusted gross estate. If Mr. Smith placed his home, bank accounts and securities in joint names with his wife, the marital deduction is still limited to one-half of his adjusted gross estate. On the death of Mrs. Smith, however, all the assets she received from Mr. Smith, together with other assets which she owns, will be taxed in her estate without benefit of a full marital deduction at her husband's death.

If Mr. Smith's estate amounted to about $200,000, all of which was held jointly with his wife, the tax on his death would be approximately $4,500. The tax on Mrs. Smith's death after his, however, even assuming she had no assets of her own, would amount to approximately $28,000; the total federal estate tax paid by both estates would be about $32,500. If Mr. Smith had not placed the property in joint names, but instead had left one-half of his property to his wife under his will and left the other to a trust (which could pay the income and, at the discretion of the trustees, trust principal to his wife), the tax on Mr. Smith's death would remain at approximately $4,500. The tax on his wife's estate would also approximate $4,500; the total tax in both estates would then be something less than $9,000. This would result in almost $25,000 less tax than that payable if Mr. Smith placed all of his assets in joint names.

Placing property in joint names with a third party may also result in unintended or excessive generosity. Mr. Miller, for instance, wishing to see that his nephew is adequately provided for without (he thought) depriving his wife and children in any way, placed a savings account containing approximately $25,000 in his own name and that of his nephew. At the time he does this, Mr. Miller's estate is approximately $225,000; during the succeeding years, however, as a result of business reverses and costly medical expenses, Mr. Miller's probate estate dwindles to $50,000. Since Mr. Miller's will directed that all taxes and expenses be paid out of his residuary estate, the nephew receives the $25,000 free and clear, while Mr. Miller's widow and children all together, after debts, funeral expenses, taxes and fees are paid out of the estate, receive only about $20,000.

Mr. Armstrong's property also wound up in unexpected hands although he was not around to witness it. He placed all of his property in joint names with his wife. After his death, his young wife remarried a pleasant young man named Mr. Baker. She was so impressed by the ease with which she received the jointly held property that she placed all of it in the joint names of herself and Mr. Baker. Upon Mrs. Armstrong's untimely death, Mr. Baker became the owner of all her property, and although still a pleasant fellow, he saw no need to spend any of it for the benefit of Mr. Armstrong's now teenage children.

The two preceding examples show that the unthinking use of joint ownership may give rise to problems in addition to, and perhaps even more serious than, the tax difficulties which also may arise from the use of joint ownership.

One aspect of a decision to place property in joint names of which many people are unaware is that a gift tax can be incurred. When Mr. Dunkin generously places all of his securities in joint names with his unmarried sister, he may unwittingly find himself liable for a substantial gift tax. Moreover, upon his death, the securities will be subject to federal estate tax even though he has had to pay the gift tax. The credit his estate may receive for the gift tax is small consolation.

One final example shows some of the unintended and unpredictable consequences which can arise as the result of joint ownership. The bank account set up for a favorite niece can grow to a substantial figure, and then the niece can die. The niece has accumulated her own estate and her personal representative finds among her effects in her safe deposit box the pass book for the joint account created by old Uncle Ned, who is still living. The title of the account is "Uncle Ned, in trust for himself and niece Jane, joint owners, subject to the order of either; the balance at the death of either to belong to the survivor."

Who owns the bank account? Uncle Ned created it; Jane did not deposit a dime into the account; and upon review it is determined that the only withdrawal ever made was by Jane one year before her death, in the amount of $4,000 (the balance was $10,000 at death). Further investigation showed that with the $4,000 she bought ten shares of IBM stock, which at her death was 20 shares with a value of $7,000. The IBM stock was registered "Niece Jane, in trust for herself and Uncle Ned, joint owners, subject to the order of either; the balance at the death of either to belong to the survivor." The stock certificate was also found in her safe deposit box.

What does the personal representative do? Under Maryland law, the bank account and the IBM stock clearly belong to Uncle Ned. However, Jane's personal representative is going to have to report both of these assets in her federal estate tax return, and Internal Revenue Service will require him to prove (or to pay tax on these assets):

1. That the funds in the savings account consist solely of assets contributed by Uncle Ned (and there may be a different rule regarding the interest earned on the account);

2. That the delivery of the savings account book to niece Jane was not tantamount to a gift, which would include the full amount of the account, notwithstanding its origin, in Jane's estate; and

3. That the registration of the IBM stock in joint names was not a gift in contemplation of death by Jane (and incidentally, she was seriously ill for three years prior to her death, but no one knows whether she was aware that she had been suffering from an incurable cancer during that time).

Neither Uncle Ned nor niece Jane filed any gift tax return prior to Jane's death. Jane reported (Uncle Ned did not) and paid income tax on all the income from the savings account and the IBM stock.

The Maryland inheritance tax collector is going to be slightly more generous as far as the bank account and stock is concerned, and will permit the payment of inheritance tax at the rate of 7 1/2% on only 1/2 of the balance of both, *unless* he decides that the purchase of the IBM stock with the proceeds of some of the savings account two years before Jane's death, and the placing of it in joint names, constituted a gift of a substantial amount which is also subject (in full) to Maryland inheritance tax.

By her will, Jane left all the rest and residue of her estate to her children. She did not mention Uncle Ned because she knew he didn't need anything from her, and she told her lawyer that she didn't want to leave Uncle Ned anything. Since her entire estate was divided up among eight children, her lawyer decided that it wasn't necessary to have any direction in the will about payment of taxes. The average tax rate on her estate is 39%.

What happens to the joint account and the IBM stock? At the very least, Uncle Ned will have to pay a tax of 39% on $7,000—the value of the IBM stock. If the Internal Revenue

Service should insist that the $10,000 balance of the savings account was a gift to Jane, he will also have to pay $3,900—39% of the balance. And, therefore, he will end up considerably worse than if he had simply tried to take care of Jane by will, avoiding the joint property ownership in the first place.

Government Bonds

Frequently U.S. bonds are registered in two or more names. A common method of registering such bonds is "John Doe or Mary Doe" (husband and wife). A problem often arises if John or Mary Doe dies. Does half the interest in these bonds pass under the decedent's will or belong to the survivor named on the bond? After conflicting court rulings in the several states, it was held by the U.S. Supreme Court in 1962 that the survivor named on the bond became the sole owner at the death of the other co-owner.

When a U.S. savings bond is registered in the name of two individuals as co-owners, either may redeem it without permission of the other. Upon the death of one, the surviving co-owner becomes the sole owner. If a bond is registered "Richard Brown, payable on death to Richard Brown, Jr.," then upon the death of Richard Brown, the named beneficiary becomes the sole owner. The bonds are not a part of the probate estate of the first to die and are not liable for payment of the decedent's debts. However, this form of registration should not be used if the person who furnishes the purchase money wants to leave the bonds to someone in his will other than the registered co-owner. And, as is all other property, these bonds too are subject to estate tax.

Bank Accounts

The most common form of joint account in Maryland is the trust form with common law right of survivorship which usually provides "AB, in trust for himself and CD, joint owners, subject to the order of either; the balance at death of either to belong to the survivor."

The existence of the trust form of account creates a rebuttable presumption that the trust is valid and the balance belongs to the survivor, but the personal representative of the deceased or other interested parties can show that the deceased did not intend that the joint owner should inherit the balance in the account. In a recent case, where there was clear evidence that the purpose of creating a joint checking account between the decedent and his landlady two days before his death was to facilitate payment of his bills, the court found that the decedent's estate and not the joint owner was entitled to the funds on the decedent's death. While the ultimate result of the case appears satisfactory, it should be remembered that it took an expensive court trial and an appeal to the Court of Appeals of Maryland to achieve it.

Since the trust survivorship account is the most common form of account, and, indeed in some banks is the only form of joint account, it is often used in circumstances where, as a matter of convenience, the owner of the account wishes to have someone else able to withdraw funds from the account. (One important reason why this is the most used form is that many banks have rubber stamps, to be used when accounts are created, with this legend on them and spaces for the names to be filled in!) The problem arises because the owner of the account may not really want the joint owner to inherit the account. But, as shown above, if the surviving joint owner claims the account, those he intended to inherite the account will be forced to file suit and try to prove in court that a survivorship account was not intended. This will involve expense, and the outcome is not at all certain.

Where it is desired to give another person the right to withdraw from a bank account, a much more satisfactory solution is for the owner to keep the account in his own name and to execute a power of attorney giving the other person power to withdraw funds during the life of the owner, but without any right of survivorship. Then, upon the owner's death, the balance in the account would pass under his will.

Summary

From the above discussion it should be clear that there is no absolute, or general, rule concerning the advisability of placing property in joint names, but that it is important for an individual to obtain professional advice before taking any such step. Joint ownership of property can reduce the original owner's complete control over the property. Since he is sharing ownership, under law, he will also share management and control of the property. This may not be a problem if the owners are harmonious, but the family picture can change through a divorce or family squabble. There may be advantages to joint ownership in certain situations. For instance, the property does pass quickly to the surviving joint tenant; in the instance of tenants by the entireties, it may reduce Maryland inheritance tax; and, in some cases, there may be added protection against creditors. In general, however, the disadvantages of joint ownership outweigh the advantages. As a result, before placing substantial amounts of property in survivorship form, the owner should clearly understand all the effects of sharing ownership of his property prior to his death.

13

Will Substitutes— the Revocable Trust

A *trust* is the separation of the ownership of property into two parts with legal title (or management) of the property in one person and beneficial ownership of the property in another person. There are two broad categories of trusts—the living trust (sometimes called an *inter vivos* trust) and the testamentary trust. A *living trust* is created during the maker's lifetime, while a *testamentary trust* is created upon the maker's death by his will.

Further, there are two classes of living trusts, revocable and irrevocable. A *revocable trust*, as its name implies, is one that can be cancelled or changed during its existence. Withdrawal of all or part of the trust assets can be made at any time at the request of the maker of the revocable trust. An *irrevocable trust*, on the other hand, is one which cannot be altered.

It is also desirable to know the terms used in connection with trusts. The maker of a trust is the *grantor* or *settlor*. The trustee or trustees are those who are given legal title, possession and management of the trust assets. And a person who benefits from the trust is a trust *beneficiary*.

Terms of a Typical Revocable Trust

In the typical revocable living trust a grantor transfers property to a trustee or trustees under a written agreement. The agreement provides for the trustees to manage and invest the trust property and to pay the grantor all income from the trust during his lifetime, together with such amounts of principal as may be requested by the grantor. It also provides that the trustees may pay principal to or for the benefit of the grantor at any time (for example to pay for illness), and it always provides that the grantor can amend or revoke the trust at any time.

Upon the death of the grantor, the trust becomes irrevocable, meaning that the terms of the trust cannot thereafter be changed. The trust property is held, administered and distributed as if it had passed under the grantor's will through probate and into a testamentary trust. The provisions of the trust agreement which apply to the administration and distribution of the trust assets after the grantor's death become operative and are carried out immediately. There are no probate delays, usually less probate expense, and the publicity normally necessary to the probate of a will is dispensed with.

A revocable living trust has both a number of advantages and a number of disadvantages when compared with a testamentary trust.

Advantages of the Revocable Trust

Management Uninterrupted by Incapacity

If a bank or an experienced person or both are selected as trustees of a revocable living trust and a large part of all of the grantor's assets are placed in the trust during his lifetime, the revocable trust can afford continuous experienced management of the trust assets regardless of the grantor's physical or mental incapacity. If the grantor desires to retain investment control of the trust assets, the trust agreement can provide that while the grantor is alive and remains competent, no purchase or sales of the trust assets or any other important actions can be made without his approval. Should the grantor become unable to manage his assets, either through mental or physical disabilities, the revocable trust is a convenient instrument for continuing proper management.

Of course, a power of attorney given to another person to manage the grantor's affairs will be a much simpler technique if the power of attorney specifically provides, as is now permitted by Maryland law (see Chapter 18), that the power shall continue to be operative despite the grantor's incapacity. If neither a revocable trust nor this type of power of attorney is executed, proceedings for the appointment of a guardian for the property of a person upon his becoming senile or incompetent, or upon his drifting in and out of lucid mental periods, may become necessary. These can provoke unpleasant family quarrels and will also require the trouble and expense of court proceedings.

The revocable living trust is one answer to these problems. The trustees can perform all of the necessary management of the trust assets, including the collection of income, the purchase and sale of trust assets and the management of real estate or a closely held business. In addition, the trustees can make payment of hospital, nursing and doctors' bills and other expenses of the grantor. When the period of temporary crisis ends, the trust can be revoked by the grantor if he so desires, or the grantor may again take up active management of his trust assets while leaving the assets with the trustees. If the grantor dies, the trust can act as the grantor's will insofar as the assets of the trust are concerned.

Pour Over of Probate Assets

One of the advantages of a revocable trust is that it can operate during the grantor's lifetime with respect to certain assets of his that he wishes to have managed by trustees, and at the same time serve as a vehicle into which his other assets which pass under his will can be "poured" when he dies. If an individual decides to set up a revocable trust, it is not wise to have separate trusts functioning for the same purposes after his death. Therefore, if he sets up a living trust in which he provides for his wife and children after his death, he is frequently advised by his lawyer that upon his death any property which is not included in the trust, such as additional securities and any other investment property, would pass by his will to the trustees of his revocable trust. Life insurance, too, can pass to these trustees by written instructions issued during life to the insurance company. This makes it unnecessary for him to have an elaborate will paralleling the provisions of his trust and (once again) avoids the publicity attendant upon probate. True, the curious would know the extent of his probate estate, but they would not know too much about the value of his aggregate estate, nor would they know what disposition he ultimately made of his assets. One who is both curious and clever could probably work backward from the amount of federal estate tax paid, which would be disclosed in the probate proceeding, but most people are not quite that energetic.

Management for the Busy Executive or Professional

A revocable trust is a valuable aid to the busy executive or professional person who does not have time to study the stock market or to do the many other things involved in managing the investment of valuable trust assets. Expert trustees can supply experienced investment guidance and free a busy executive or professional person from the worries that might interfere with the pursuit of his business or profession, while at the same time assuring him of continuous investment management of his trust assets. It is true, of course, that much the same investment guidance can be obtained without a trust by using an investment counselor or through an agency account at a bank.

Trial Run for the Trustees

The revocable living trust allows the grantor to observe the operation of those he has selected to manage his estate upon his death. The grantor can then satisfy himself as to the manner in which his assets are likely to be managed and administered after his death. This will also allow his wife to become familiar with the trustees he has selected and with his lawyer (who, if qualified, is frequently one of the trustees) so that old friends, instead of strangers, will be there to take care of his wife at his death.

Privacy of Disposition of Assets at Death

Another advantage of the revocable trust is the privacy afforded the grantor in disposing of his estate at his death. Assets placed in a revocable living trust do not become a matter of public court record, as is the case with a probated will. Newspaper publicity about the grantor's assets, his beneficiaries and his disposition plans are thus avoided.

Reduction of Probate Expense

A revocable living trust may result in the reduction of probate expenses. Executor's commissions, attorney's fees, accounting fees, appraiser's fees and other charges arising from the administration of a deceased person's estate are based to a certain extent on the value of the assets passing under the decedent's will. Keeping property out of the grantor's probate or testamentary estate can reduce some of these charges. If all of a grantor's assets are in a revocable trust at the time of his death, it is possible, though this would be rare, that probate may not be necessary at all. However, this reduction of probate expenses will be offset to a greater or lesser degree by the commissions paid to the trustee during the grantor's lifetime, depending on the trust's duration and other factors. It could even be that the actual costs of the trust over the years would be larger than the probate costs.

Also, trust companies serving as trustees under a living trust ofter require that the trust agreement contain provisions for the payment of additional compensation to the trustee over and above the commissions set by law, to which testamentary trustees are usually limited, unless the will also provides for such extra compensation. These extra charges are designed to compensate the trustees for such services as making the necessary investigations for the careful exercise of discretionary powers (such as the payment of principal for a beneficiary) or for performing certain duties upon the grantor's death for which, if the probate estate is small, the trustees cannot otherwise be adequately compensated. While this extra expense is usually reasonable and justified, it does tend, of course, to offset the saving in probate expenses resulting from a revocable trust.

In any event, the possible saving of probate expenses is only one of many factors which should be considered in each individual case in weighing the relative merits of a revocable living trust and a testamentary trust.

Uninterrupted Management at Death

A revocable living trust provides a means for avoiding any interruption in the management of the trust's assets upon the death of the grantor. Stocks, securities, real estate and so on can continue to be managed without interruption. Further, there is no delay incurred in providing for the grantor's family immediately after his death. This elimination of delay may be important if the trust property consists of assets which require day-to-day handling to avoid loss and when the family has immediate financial requirements upon the death of the grantor. On the other hand, the new Maryland probate laws permit equally prompt action by a skillful personal representative.

Avoidance of Probate in Other States

If the grantor owns property located in different states, it may be possible to avoid expensive and time-consuming probate proceedings in these states by conveying the property to a trustee during the grantor's lifetime. However, if real estate in other states is to be placed in a revocable living trust, it is important to make sure that the laws of the state where the property is located allow a trustee from another state to act within that state. Maryland law is very liberal in this regard; some other states (for example, Virginia) have other ideas.

Tax Treatment of the Revocable Trust

Assets in a revocable living trust are taxable under the federal income and estate tax laws and the Maryland income and inheritance tax laws in the same manner as property which the grantor continues to own outright. No gift tax however, is payable when a grantor creates a revocable living trust. During his lifetime all trust income is taxed to him, and upon his death all of the property in the trust is included in his estate for federal estate and Maryland inheritance tax purposes. As in a will, the assets in the revocable living trust acquire an income tax basis equal to their fair market value at the grantor's death, or as otherwise determined for federal estate tax purposes in the grantor's estate. After his death the trust becomes irrevocable and is taxed in the same manner as a testamentary trust. There may be some income tax disadvantages to a funded revocable trust because the opportunity to use the estate as a separate tax-paying entity may be reduced. This matter is discussed at the end of Chapter 20.

Avoidance of Will Contest

A revocable trust is less vulnerable to attack by disgruntled heirs than is a will. It is rather easy for an heir to attack the probate of a will, even when the attack is based on flimsy reasons. It is often expensive and time consuming for the personal representative to win a total victory in such a contest.

Since the decedent's heirs are not given the same official notice of a revocable living trust as they are of the probate of the decedent's will, it is possible that a disgruntled heir will not learn of the trust's existence. Also, although a revocable living trust can be attacked on some of the same grounds used to contest a will (such as lack of mental capacity or undue influence), a living trust agreement need not be executed with the same formalities and legal requirements as a will (such as execution in the presence of two witnesses), and thus a living trust cannot be attacked merely on the ground that these formal requirements have not been satisfied.

Minimum Funding Required During Grantor's Life

A revocable living trust can serve as a useful estate planning mechanism even though it is funded by only a minimum amount of the grantor's assets during his lifetime, or perhaps even not funded with specific assets at all but with only the commitment that the proceeds of insurance policies on the grantor's life will be payable to the trust upon his death. In such situations, the trust is simply named as the recipient of the grantor's assets on his death, and his will can then be a short one devising and bequeathing the residue of his estate to the trust established under the living trust agreement. This estate planning technique insures some of the same privacy of disposition of the decedent's assets noted above and also serves as a method by which insurance proceeds can be promptly paid to the trust, which will ultimately receive the decedent's probate assets upon settlement of his estate, to be held in trust in accordance with the terms of the trust agreement. This merging of insurance proceeds and probate assets in one trust can also be accomplished by making the insurance proceeds payable to the trustees of a testamentary trust named in the will, but until rather recently insurance companies were reluctant to do this. There still could be delays and problems if the probate of the will naming the testamentary trustees is contested or delayed.

Disadvantages of the Revocable Trust

Briefly, the following (some of these points are already referred to) are some disadvantages of a revocable living trust:

Cost

The cost of a living trust may frequently equal or exceed, depending of course on the time the trust is in existence, the actual additional probate cost where the property is left in the grantor's estate and is administered by his personal representative.

Loss of Income Tax Exemption

Where there is a revocable trust, upon the death of the grantor there is a loss of an additional income tax pocket (see Chapter 20) and therefore additional income taxes to pay during the period of estate administration.

Power of Attorney May Be Advisable

In Maryland, the commissions charged by the trustees are uniform, and in some situations the far less expensive method of administration of assets under a properly drawn power of attorney under Maryland's new rules (see Chapter 18) may be preferable. The use of a power of attorney in Maryland, unlike the more stringent rule in many other states, is permitted even during periods of disability. In many cases this will sharply reduce the cost of temporary or even long-term management of the affairs of an incompetent or ill person.

Amendment or Termination of a Revocable Trust

Although in the hands of sophisticated grantors and lawyers this may not always be a serious problem, nevertheless the amendment or termination of a revocable deed of trust is somewhat more ponderous and time consuming than the preparation of a codicil or a new will. Additional steps—approval of the trustee, execution of necessary papers amending or terminating the trust, reregistration of securities, etc., are in contrast to the simplicity of preparation and execution of a codicil or a will which can partly or totally change the plan of disposition of an estate. For example, a codicil or a new will can be made anywhere in the world without the approval of anyone else through the simple procedure of preparing the instrument and executing it before witnesses in accordance with the law of Maryland or the law of the location where the will is made.

Summary

A revocable living trust frequently is a very useful tool for management of assets of a living individual. The question of whether or not one should execute such a trust requires a study of all the possibilities, of the desires and intentions of the person, of the costs involved, and all other relevant factors, many of which are outlined in this chapter. In each case an attorney should be consulted, and together the lawyer and his client should study all of the problems, possibilities and solutions.

14
Will Substitutes—
Life Insurance

Life insurance is a unique and important asset. It forms the bulk of many estates and is an important supplementary asset in others. Over the years, laws have been passed at both the state and federal levels which encourage the purchase of life insurance policies and which confer significant tax and non-tax benefits.

Exemption from Creditors

One of the most substantial benefits given to policy holders by Maryland law is that the proceeds of life insurance payable to or for the benefit of a man's wife, children, dependent relatives, or any combination of the three, are exempt from the claims of all creditors. Thus, even if a man dies leaving a mountain of debts or a lawsuit resulting in a judgment against his estate, his life insurance would be available to support his widow and children if he named them as beneficiaries of the policies.

There are only minor exceptions to this policy of the law. The two principal exceptions are (1) if the insured borrows money and specifically pledges a life insurance policy as security for the debt, a creditor can collect his debt out of the proceeds of that policy, and (2) an insured may not validly change the beneficiary of his policies or assign ownership of them with actual intent to hinder, delay or defraud his creditors.

Maryland Inheritance Tax Advantages

The other major benefit given to policy holders by Maryland law is that the proceeds of life insurance payable to any beneficiary *other than* the estate or personal representative of the insured are not subject to Maryland inheritance tax. Interestingly enough, there is no specific statute in Maryland granting this exemption. However, the Attorney General of Maryland ruled insurance proceeds exempt from the inheritance tax at least as far back as 1937, and this ruling has been acquiesced in by the tax authorities throughout the state.

In some situations it may be best not to take full advantage of this inheritance tax exemption. Death creates a need for cash. If there is no other ready source of sufficient cash, it may be wise to make a small or even moderate amount of insurance proceeds, say $5,000-$10,000, specifically payable (in writing on company forms) to "the estate of the insured" to provide the needed liquidity, even though the proceeds so paid will be computed in arriving at a 1% or 7 1/2% Maryland inheritance tax which is assessed against all amounts distributed to legatees (except charities, churches, etc.).

Types of Life Insurance Policies

There are many types of life insurance policies, but the two most important to the average person are ordinary life and term policies. The *ordinary life policy* is a permanent contract with a fixed annual or periodic cost to the purchaser which is calculated on his age at the time he takes out his policy. Since the obligations of a man age 60 may be much less than they were when he was, say, age 35—his children have grown up and left home, his house has been paid for, and he is investing more in other assets—there may come a time when he decides to stop paying premiums on his ordinary life policy. At that time, he can then elect to take paid-up insurance for a small face amount of proceeds, or he may surrender some of his policies for their cash values.

The *term policy* is paid for at a fixed rate during each term (1 to 5 years) for which it is purchased. It is initially cheaper than ordinary life insurance, but it costs increasingly more to renew as each term expires, since the owner is older and more likely to die during the particular term for which the company has agreed to take the risk. Term insurance is more and more being recognized as a valuable estate planning tool.

In today's society a very popular form of term policy is group term life insurance available through one's employer, labor union, or through the trustees of a fund established by the employer or labor union. For many years Maryland had a statute restricting the amount of group life insurance which an employer, etc., could issue to any one person. In 1971, all ceilings on the amount of group life insurance which can cover the life of any employee were repealed.

Another statute regulating group term life policies gives an employee who terminates his employment the valuable right to purchase individual insurance, without evidence of insurability, within 31 days after he terminates his employment.

Methods of Paying Proceeds

Besides knowing to whom he wants life insurance proceeds paid, the insured must decide how he wants them paid. Life insurance policies provide at least four principal settlement options at death, in addition to the option of a single lump sum payment.

Under the *interest option* the beneficiary leaves the death proceeds with the insurance company. The company will pay the beneficiary interest on a monthly, quarterly, semi-annual, annual or other periodic basis. Companies usually guarantee some minimum rate of return (such as 2%), but in fact they will usually pay the beneficiary interest at a substantially higher rate than the minimum guaranteed rate. In addition to interest, this option gives the beneficiary the right to withdraw part or all of the proceeds from time to time.

The *fixed period option* again involves leaving the death proceeds with the insurance company. The company then pays the beneficiary a sum of money in a fixed number of installments—such as in 10 annual installments or in 240 monthly installments. Each payment consists partly of a distribution of the death proceeds and partly of interest earned on the proceeds held by the company. If the company is told how long the beneficiary wants the proceeds to last, it can calculate the number of payments the beneficiary can take out over that period and how much each payment will be.

The *fixed amount option* is quite similar to the fixed period option. The difference is that under this option the amount of each payment will remain the same even though the number of installments may increase or decrease as the total proceeds on hand or interest rates fluctuate. There are other advantages of this option over the fixed period option, and in general it is more flexible both for the beneficiary and for the company.

Finally, there is the *life annuity option*. Once again, the company keeps the proceeds and pays out in installments a total amount (including proceeds and interest earned on proceeds) based on the life expectancy of the beneficiary. Almost all companies today will guarantee the widow (or her estate) a minimum number of installments, such as 120 or 240 monthly payments. Care should be taken to see that such a minimum guaranteed number of payments is part of the option, thereby guarding against a forfeiture of a valuable property right because of the premature death of the first beneficiary.

Who Decides How Proceeds Are to Be Paid?

Being the flexible tool that it is, insurance can be set up so that either the husband during his lifetime or his widow after his death can be given the power to decide how the policy proceeds will come to her. Who should have the power depends on the financial situation of the family at the husband's death and on the ability of the widow either to make the best decision after her husband's death or to obtain the best advice available.

It is difficult for a man at age 30 to decide what will be best for his widow at age 70. Therefore, in most cases it is better to let the widow decide after the husband's death since she can make the decision based on the circumstances at that time. Yet, there may be other situations in which the husband should exercise the power to select a mode of settlement. If the wife is incapacitated (mentally or physically), or has no business judgment, or is a spendthrift, it is conceivable the husband may wish to select the option during his lifetime. If the husband makes such a decision during his lifetime, he should review the matter continually to make sure that the option he has selected is still in tune with the realities of his family's situation. Generally summarized, it can be said that there are very few instances where the husband should make an irrevocable decision to leave the proceeds with the insurance company.

A Life Insurance Trust

Instead of selecting one of the four principal options described above whereby the insurance company pays out the proceeds according to a prearranged plan, the husband can actually create a trust and name the trustee as beneficiary of the insurance proceeds.

A trust, either created before death or by will, is often advisable where the husband wishes additional flexibility and wide discretion for the trustee who will assist his widow after death. While an insurance company's settlement options offer flexibility to meet some of the business and human problems which will arise after the husband's death, the insurance company cannot use its discretion to change the amount of money to be spent for each child's unique health, education or support needs. In summary, creating a trust and naming the trustee as beneficiary of life insurance policies gives an insured not merely the opportunity to select from among four fixed choices but rather the chance to devise an estate plan which is tailor-made for his situation.

Federal Tax Considerations

Besides being affected by Maryland law and by the provisions of the insurance contract itself, insurance is also affected by the federal tax laws. The effects of three different taxes must be considered and analyzed separately—the federal estate tax, the federal gift tax and the federal income tax.

The encouragement which the law in general gives to insurance often leads people to make the erroneous assumption that "all insurance is nontaxable." It comes as a shock to them that this generality is wrong, and that there are usually tax problems connected with insurance just as with any other asset. Sometimes people who assume that all insurance is nontaxable are thinking of the exemption given from the Maryland inheritance tax. Then too, when a person says "life insurance isn't part of my estate," he usually means that life insurance on his own life is not usually part of his probate estate (that is, his estate subject to administration) but he is overlooking the fact that life insurance is possibly, and quite probably, a part of his gross estate for federal estate tax purposes.

Federal Estate Tax

To end this confusion, one must fully understand the fundamental rule that the proceeds of all insurance on the life of the insured are includible in a decedent's gross estate for federal estate tax purposes if the decedent possessed any of the incidents of ownership at the time of his death. "Incidents of ownership" is a tax term which includes, for example, the right of the insured or his estate to the economic benefits of the policy, the power to change the beneficiary, to surrender or cancel the policy, to assign it, to revoke an assignment, to pledge it for a loan, or to surrender the policy for its cash value, etc. If the decedent possesses any incident of ownership, the policy is includible in his gross estate regardless of who the beneficiary is. Even if the decedent has given up all incidents of ownership in favor of someone else, the proceeds will still be included in his gross estate if the gift is made in "contemplation of death," or if the policy is made payable to his estate.

Federal Gift Tax

In every insurance policy there are at least four participants: the owner of the policy, the insured, the insurer and the beneficiary. Typically, a husband-father is both the owner of and the insured person under a policy, but this does not have to be the case. Ownership of an insurance policy, like ownership of other assets, can be transferred or given away. For a husband with enough property to be concerned about the estate tax at his death, the impact of that tax is often a powerful incentive to give away his insurance policies to other members of his family during life and thereby eliminate the estate tax which would otherwise be payable on the proceeds of the policies. Remember that we are talking about an *absolute assignment of ownership* of a policy, not about a change of beneficiary. From what has been said above with regard to the federal estate tax, it follows that the insured can eliminate the proceeds from his gross estate for federal estate tax purposes only by making an absolute gift of every right, power, privilege and of all incidents of ownership in the policy. If he is primarily interested in protecting his wife and children, he might transfer the ownership of the policy to his wife, or to a trustee for the benefit of his wife and children. Of course, he may transfer ownership to anyone else instead (such as his church or college). No one, should make a gift of a life insurance policy, however, without thorough consideration with his attorney of all the estate planning implications.

Gifts of policies are subject to the federal gift tax. The value of a life insurance policy for gift tax purposes is the cost of replacing it on the date of the gift. Usually, this latter value is much smaller than the face amount of the policy and is the amount known as "the interpolated terminal reserve." This amount is roughly the cash surrender value of the policy, plus dividends accrued up through the date on which the policy is given, plus the proportionate part of the last premium which covers the period beyond the date of the gift. Thus, if a gift is wise for other reasons, it is often possible to eliminate tens of thousands of dollars of insurance proceeds from one's taxable estate at the cost of paying a gift tax, and perhaps no tax at all, on a few hundred or a few thousand dollars of present value.

Gifts of Life Insurance to a Trust

Instead of giving an insurance policy to his wife or to one or more of his children, the husband can create a life insurance trust and make an absolute gift of the insurance policy on his life to the trustee. He may direct the trustee to pay the income from the trust to his wife for her life, with the proceeds continuing in trust for the benefit of his children after the wife's death for a certain number of years, or with the proceeds going outright to his adult children after the wife's death. He can give the life insurance trustee the power and the right to lend funds to his estate or to buy assets from his estate.

After giving away a life insurance policy on his life, the husband-father can—with some risk of a fight with Internal Revenue—continue to pay the premiums on the policies given away. However, since there has been an historic and continuing debate for over a generation between Internal Revenue Service and taxpayers concerning the tax effects of so doing, the husband should seek competent legal advice before continuing to pay the premiums on these policies. At the present time it seems wise either to have the donee (recipient) pay the premiums, or else to give away not only the policies but also enough money to enable the donee to pay the premiums directly. Or he can (after full consideration of all pros and cons) give away paid-up policies or group policies on which the premiums are paid by his employer.

Federal Income Tax

Congress has conferred two very useful income tax benefits to the beneficiaries of life insurance proceeds.

First of all, the proceeds themselves are exempt from income tax. It makes no difference how the beneficiary receives the proceeds (e.g., in a lump sum, 240 monthly installments or a life annuity) or how many premiums were paid by the insured. Notice that the actual premiums paid for a $10,000 10-year paid-up policy will be much less than the $10,000 face amount. No income tax is due on the considerable economic gain which has resulted. (Again, however, the reader must be cautioned about a very difficult problem affected by what is called the "transfer for value" rule; counsel must be consulted in all cases.) There is a very large interest factor being built up and compounded over the life of the insured to enable the insurance company to pay off the proceeds at his death. This is like putting money into a savings account and compounding the interest over the years. (Indeed, whole life insurance is sometimes likened to a "forced savings account.") With a savings account, however, income tax is paid each year on the interest earned. Not so with a life insurance policy. Although largely unheralded today and perhaps unappreciated in advance of the receipt of death proceeds, it is a true advantage of insurance over other assets.

The second income tax benefit is conferred only on widows or widowers. If a surviving spouse takes one of the installment options under a life policy (fixed period, fixed amount or an annuity option) the insuring company is contractually obligated to pay interest on the proceeds which it holds. Interest on insurance proceeds, unlike the proceeds themselves, are subject to income tax, just like interest from any other asset. Remember that each payment from the insurance company under one of the installment or annuity options will consist partly of tax-free insurance proceeds and partly of taxable interest on the proceeds. The benefit which Congress has conferred is to allow the widow (or widower) to exclude from his income up to $1,000 in interest per year which is earned on proceeds left with the company. For example, if the widow or widower receives $1,800 in interest in a given year, he or she may exclude $1,000 and report only $800. Again, only the surviving spouse, not any other beneficiary, is eligible for this second tax benefit. Also, this tax benefit does not apply if the beneficiary elects the interest-only option.

How Should the Widow Take the Proceeds?

Although this is one of the most important decisions she must make, there is no one right answer to the question of how the widow should take the proceeds. Most widows should at least consider taking enough of the proceeds through an installment option to generate $1,000 per year in interest income (the first $1,000 per year being tax-exempt), but that is different from saying that her decision should always be affirmative. There is an easy formula which insurance companies will furnish to use in computing the amount which must be left with the insurance company under an installment option to take full advantage of the annual $1,000 income tax exclusion. Where an insurance company pays 4 to 4 1/2% under a policy and the widow receives that interest tax free, it would be difficult to find a better rate of return on taxable interest. In addition, the tax-free interest is guaranteed and the principal is safer than in other investments. However, these are not the only considerations, and a sound decision can only be made after consultation with the widow's lawyer.

After deciding whether to elect an installment option on some of her husband's life insurance policies so as to take advantage of the $1,000 annual income tax exclusion, the widow must still decide whether to take any remaining insurance proceeds in a lump sum or to elect an installment option. Most insurance companies currently guarantee 2 1/4 to 3% on their payments and actually pay 4 to 4 1/2% or more. Another alternative is to invest the proceeds in corporate stock or other securities, but this entails a greater risk and a much higher degree of management and vigilance. If the widow has received from her husband nothing of substance except a modest amount of insurance proceeds and cannot be certain that what she has will be enough to provide for her no matter how long she lives, she should probably select an installment option for the proceeds, such as a life annuity, even though she might be able to make more money in other investments. She should not forget, however, that any such decision is irrevocable, and she can't thereafter ask the insurance company to give her more even in case of illness or other serious emergency.

Summary

Life insurance means using funds now to provide for later needs. The principal factor working against building an estate is lack of time. Life insurance provides an "instant estate" and allows the tax-free accumulation of interest to create the capital. If one lives long enough and saves enough and doesn't pay income taxes on interest being earned, he can accumulate the means to provide for his later years and the welfare of his family. If he dies prematurely, life insurance takes the place of the time he lost and helps to assure the financial welfare of his family.

15

Probate and Tax Savings Through Gifts

Aside from any tax considerations, gifts often play a part in passing property from one generation to the next. Parents may transfer an interest in the family business to their children in order to increase the children's interest in the enterprise and to equip them to assume the responsibilities of management. Husbands sometimes place securities in trust to assure income for their wives. Parents may do the same for the protection of their children.

Possible Savings

In addition, gifts may have the effect of reducing income and estate taxes, as well as lowering the costs of probate. In planning gifts, however, the welfare of the person making the gift and the welfare of the one receiving it should be the paramount considerations. An older person should not make gifts which would impair his security, his capacity to provide for himself or his opportunity to continue useful and gainful employment. A child should not be given funds or property which he is too young to handle. The selection and timing of gifts to young people who lack experience in financial management should be designed to further their proper training and development, with adequate provisions for the care and management of property. The desire to effect tax savings or to avoid probate costs should be secondary. It is better to provide for the payment of taxes and other costs by purchasing additional life insurance or by some other method than to make gifts which would prejudice the security of the giver or be unsuited to the position of the receiver.

There are a number of different ways that gifts may be made. If gifts are made to a minor or to an incompetent, a guardian may be appointed by a court of his or her residence to administer the estate of the recipient. Recent statutes have been enacted in Maryland which greatly simplify gifts to minors and under which gifts of any kind of real or personal property may be made to a custodian who holds the property for a minor. In addition, there are various types of trusts to be considered.

Gifts to Guardians

Under Maryland's modern and broad act for making gifts to minors through a custodian, it would be a rare case today when anyone would make any kind of a gift outright to a minor which would require the expense and formality of a court-appointed guardian.

Even if a guardian had been appointed for a person who is mentally or physically unable to take care of his affairs, it is doubtful that a living person would need to make a gift to an incompetent, or through his guardian. If such a person wished to assist the incompetent, he could pay his expenses directly to the person taking care of the incompetent, or he could create a trust for his benefit.

However, a gift to a guardian of a minor or incompetent under Maryland's modern and flexible guardianship laws would receive the protection of the court appointing the guardian, and yet the guardian would have almost the same powers of management and disposition as a trustee under a trust arrangement.

Guardianships in Maryland today are neither expensive nor cumbersome, but still, gifts to guardians, or gifts requiring guardianship, are not favored.

Custodial Arrangements

Most states have adopted the Uniform Gifts to Minors Act, but the act is limited in most of those states to gifts of securities, life insurance policies, annuity contracts and money. However, in 1969 Maryland adopted its own revised act, which permits gifts of any type of property by an adult to minors under the supervision of a named custodian, who may be the donor, any other adult or a trust company.

The procedure for establishing a custodial arrangement is very simple. It does not have to be administered by any court, no surety bond is required of the custodian, and no compensation need be paid the custodian, unless the donor so directs.

The custodian has broad powers of management and may pay over to the minor, or expend for the minor's benefit, as much of the custodial property, including the income, as the custodian in his discretion deems advisable for the minor's support, maintenance and education. When the minor attains the age of 21, the custodial property must be delivered to him.

In most cases a transfer of property to a minor pursuant to either the Uniform Gifts to Minors Act or the Maryland version is considered a completed gift for tax purposes. The income from the custodial property would thereafter belong to the minor under the income tax laws of the United States and Maryland. The Internal Revenue Service has ruled, however, that the income from such property, to the extent it is used for the minor's support, is includible in the gross income of any person who is legally obligated to support the minor. The property would not be taxable in the donor's estate if he lives for three years after the gift. But the property would be includible in the gross estate of the donor if he appoints himself custodian and dies while serving in that capacity and before the minor becomes 21. Therefore, a parent who makes gifts to minor children through this vehicle should almost never name himself as custodian.

Gifts in Trusts

The indirect gift, the gift in trust, should be considered a device for lifetime giving where the property given needs expert management, or the amount involved warrants the services of a trustee, or the donor wants the arrangement to continue after the beneficiary reaches age 21 in the case of a gift to a minor. In a trust arrangement, the giver can specify the rules to be applied to the management and use of the property or the income from it. The terms of the trust may be more or less stringent than a guardianship or custodial arrangement, and provisions may be inserted for many eventualities.

The preparation of the trust document, since it is an agreement with many legal implications, requires the services of an attorney. Even where gifts of mutual fund shares are made through trust agreements prepared by the company selling such shares, the giver should still seek the advice of his attorney, who can advise him as to all tax consequences of such a trust agreement, and whether all of his objectives will be attained.

The expense involved in the establishment and thereafter in the operation of a trust must be given thoughtful consideration and compared with such expenses under custodial arrangements or guardianship.

Gift Tax Considerations

Since property passing from one person to another by gift is ordinarily free from federal estate taxes, a federal gift tax has been enacted to prevent excessive avoidance of the estate tax through gifts. Usually the gift tax is less than the estate tax, and gift tax brackets are lower for comparable amounts of property. Estate money used to pay the estate tax is subject to taxation, but money used to pay a gift tax reduces the estate by the amount paid.

Gifts made within three years of death are presumed to be in contemplation of death. If the donor's personal representative does not disprove this, such gifts will still be a part of the taxable estate. However, in computing the estate tax a credit based on the amount of gift tax previously paid is allowed. If the gift tax is not paid prior to death (thereby reducing the estate), an estate tax deduction may be claimed for the liability to pay the gift tax. For this reason, there is usually some overall tax savings even if a gift is held to be in contemplation of death.

The Annual Exclusion

There are two provisions in the gift tax statutes under which gifts are free from tax altogether. The annual exclusion provision permits a person to make a tax-free gift of cash or property worth up to $3,000 to each of any number of people each year. This provision was inserted to permit normal gifts (for example wedding presents), and periodic gifts such as birthday and Christmas presents. Thus, a single person wishing to give a total of $9,000 each year, tax free, can do so if he divides the gifts among three recipients.

Since husband and wife may combine their exclusions, as much as $6,000 can be given to each recipient each year. For example, a married couple owning substantial amounts of corporate stock and having four children could give $24,000 worth of stock to their children each year. Over a period of 20 years they could divest themselves, tax free, of $480,000 worth of stock. Allowing for ordinary appreciation, the amount removed from their estates might be substantially greater when valued at the end of the 20-year period. The power of a husband and wife to combine their exclusions applies even though the property given might be separately owned only by one of them. Again a warning: look out first for the security of the giver!

To qualify for the annual exclusion the terms of transferring gifts to minors must meet the following conditions:

1. Both the property and its income may be expended by, or for the benefit of, the minor prior to his attaining the age of 21. The amount not so expended must pass to him at that time.

2. In the event of the donee's death prior to age 21, the property and income not expended will pass to his estate or to persons appointed by his will under the exercise of a general power of appointment.

Still another fundamental to be borne in mind regarding the gift tax is that the annual exclusion is usually not available with gifts in trust involving "future interests," that is, gifts which do not meet points 1 and 2 above, if enjoyment of the gift is postponed until after age 21. The annual exclusion will, however, be available where a gift is made to a custodian for the benefit of a minor.

The annual exclusion may also be used when gifts are made to a trust which can be revoked by the beneficiary. For tax purposes such gifts are considered equivalent to outright gifts to be beneficiary, provided he is a competent adult.

The Lifetime Exemption

The other provision relating to tax-free gifts is called the lifetime exemption. It permits a person to give away a total of $30,000 during his lifetime (in the case of husband and wife, $60,000) in addition to the annual exclusion. The lifetime gift tax exemption was originally enacted to permit a larger gift, such as a transfer of an interest in a family business. The provision is now less effective in achieving this objective due to increases in property values measured in dollars since the statute was enacted. Nevertheless, beginning gift tax rates are relatively low, and husband and wife can make a gift of $100,000, in addition to their annual exclusion gifts, and pay a tax of only $2,400.

The lifetime exemption may be used partly at one time and partly at another, and it may be used for a gift to one person or for gifts divided among several. A single person could give $33,000 in one year to one person, or $13,000 in each of three years to one person, or $8,000 in one year to each of six persons before exhausting his lifetime gift privileges. Once the amount of the lifetime exemption has been utilized, however, it is no longer available.

How the Tax Is Computed

The gift tax is computed on a cumulative basis. When taxable gifts are made, the amount of the tax is determined by calculating the total taxable gifts made in the current and previous years and subtracting the tax paid on the previous gifts. For this reason gift tax brackets increase as taxable gifts are made. Assume a single person who has exhausted his annual exclusions and lifetime exemptions by other gifts makes a taxable gift in 1971 of $20,000. The gift tax on this would be $1,200, or 6% of the amount given. If an additional gift is made in 1972, of which $20,000 is taxable, the tax in 1972 will be computed in the following way:

Total taxable gifts made to date	$40,000
Gift tax on $40,000 of taxable gifts	$3,600
Less gift tax previously paid	−1,200
Gift tax due on $20,000 given in 1972	$2,400

The second $20,000 has, therefore, been taxed at 12%. The gift tax brackets increase progressively until the bracket of 57.75% is reached. In the case of married persons, since the amount of taxable gifts may be divided between them, the escalation into the higher brackets progresses at half the rate of single persons.

Maryland Taxes

Maryland does not impose any tax on gifts made by living donors during their lifetime. However, Maryland will impose an inheritance tax on any gift made in contemplation of death or intended to take effect in possession or enjoyment at or after the death of the giver, including jointly owned property (except between spouses) and any property over which the donor retained any dominion during his lifetime. This same law defines dominion as the reservation of a beneficial interest in favor of the donor or of a power of revocation absolute or conditional or of a power of appointment by will or otherwise over the property. Also, any transfer of a material part of the donor's property in the nature of a final disposition or distribution made by the giver within two years prior to his death is deemed to have been made in contemplation of death by the Maryland tax law, unless contrary evidence can be shown.

Therefore, to insure that no tax will be imposed by Maryland on any gift after two years, the Maryland resident must place the property beyond his own recall, control and dominion during his lifetime.

Since the income from any completed gift which would qualify for the annual exclusion under the federal gift tax law would no longer (as far as the donor is concerned) be subject to the federal income tax, it would likewise not be subject to the Maryland income tax.

Primary Considerations in Making a Gift

Although it will necessitate utilizing part of the lifetime exemption, or even perhaps the payment of some gift tax, it is often better not to limit the provisions of a trust so as to qualify for the annual exclusion. Since the interests of family members or other trust beneficiaries are the paramount consideration, it is best to incorporate into a trust those provisions which satisfy the appropriate family plan, even if it requires using the lifetime exemption or paying some gift tax.

In any event, if property given in trust is to be removed from the estate of the donor for estate tax purposes, the gift must be irrevocable, and the donor must part with the right to receive income from it. Furthermore, the donor must forego the right to determine the way in which trust benefits will be shared among the beneficiaries. He cannot reserve or retain the right, either alone or in conjunction with others, to designate who shall possess or enjoy the property or the income from it. Therefore, when estate tax considerations are important, it is desirable to use independent trustees where gifts in trust are made by living persons. The variations in arrangements which will meet the tax requirements are numerous, and the controlling rules are technical. The lawyer who drafts such instruments must develop a recommendation in each case which will comply with these rules while fulfilling family needs.

Special types of gifts may be desirable to permit a wife or child to carry insurance on the life of the father. This situation may enable the family to keep the insurance from being taxable for estate tax purposes at the father's death and still have funds available to pay taxes or for other purposes. Trusts for the purpose of owning such insurance are subject to special provisions of the tax laws which must be carefully considered.

Where larger amounts of property are involved, other types of special arrangements may be required. It may be desirable to change the form of organization of the parents' business to create interests which are easily transferred by gift. For example, voting rights and other factors affecting stock in a family enterprise may be modified so that shares are created which are appropriate for gift purposes. In such circumstances, special consideration must be given to the effect which such stock provisions may have on the valuation of the shares. Each situation presents different problems and there is no ready-made solution for all. For this reason the development of an appropriate solution in an individual case should take into consideration the economic and tax positions of the parties, the proper management of the property, and above all the best interests of the persons involved.

16

The Irrevocable Trust

The *irrevocable trust* is one which the grantor cannot revoke or alter. The grantor of the trust gives up the right to change his mind and relinquishes the trust property either permanently or for some specific period of time. A trust created by will is, of course, irrevocable, although a type of power of revocation, usually in the form of a power to invade the principal of the trust, may be conferred upon one or more of the trust beneficiaries. The same thing is true with respect to a trust created by deed which, while fully revocable during the grantor's lifetime, continues to function beyond his death. As we shall see, however, it is sometimes (although not too often) advisable for a grantor, during his lifetime, to create a trust estate over which he retains no power of revocation. Today this is done primarily for tax purposes, either to remove the assets comprising the trust from the grantor's estate subject to federal estate tax or to insure that the income from the trust will be taxed to someone other than the grantor, or for both purposes. But few persons, if any, of less than very substantial means will be willing to, nor should they, part irrevocably with their property. A word of caution here—where there is no provision in a deed of trust expressly or impliedly reserving to the grantor power to revoke the trust, the trust is irrevocable.

Why Trusts?

Since the irrevocable trust by definition involves a more permanent form of arrangement than the revocable trust, it seems wise to consider at least briefly some basic information concerning trusts. A trust is simply a device by which the legal title to property and the right to control it are separated from the right to receive the benefits from it. Historically, the need for such a separation arose from the plight of the man with property who wanted to make provision for his family or friends but feared giving property directly to them because of their inexperience in financial management or their irresponsibility. He solved this problem by placing the legal title and management of the property in the hands of a third party whom he considered responsible. He then stipulated the manner in which the benefits were to be paid to his beneficiary.

The assurance of proper financial management is one of the more important nontax reasons for the existence of trusts. The decision as to who should be selected as trustee to exercise this management is much more important in an irrevocable trust than in a revocable trust. Sometimes a person wanting to create a trust has confidence in the judgment and managing abilities of a relative, a friend, a lawyer or a business associate. But such a person is not always available. Even if he is, he may die or become disabled or the time which he can devote to management of the trust may be too limited. For tax reasons, if an individual is a trustee he should ordinarily not be, directly or indirectly, a beneficiary of the trust.

The increasing need for reliable and capable trustees has spurred tremendous growth in the size and capability of bank

trust departments in Maryland. Almost every bank of substantial size now has a trust department. Although their skill
in managing property and investments varies, the high quality
of management in our Maryland banks and close govern-
mental supervision of bank trust department activities helps
assure certain standards of performance and inspires confidence in the integrity of banks as trustees. Grantors very
frequently find that the combination of a bank and one or
more individuals as co-trustees is an effective team, and it is
always possible to provide for successor individual trustees
for the entire life of the trust if the grantor desires it.

In addition to sound financial management, a trust offers
its grantor an opportunity for added flexibility in carrying
out his desires regarding his beneficiaries. The classic pattern
is for one beneficiary to receive all of the income for life with
the remainder paid at his death to others. The income, as well
as the remainder, can also be divided among several beneficiaries if that is desirable, and termination can occur at a time
other than death. For example, a father might create a trust
providing for distribution of the income among his children
until the youngest attains age 25. At that time the trust
would terminate, and the principal of the trust would be
divided among the children. The variations are limitless.

Even with all the possibilities open to the grantor of a
trust, he must recognize that the circumstances which inspire
his decisions today may change during the term of the trust.
The perfect plan of distribution which he creates today may
become the straitjacket of tomorrow when unexpected
events occur. A trust which irrevocably provides for the equal
division of income between two children may seem unfortunate in retrospect if one child accumulates (or marries into)
wealth and has substantial income, and the other becomes
incapacitated and incapable of supporting himself. The rec-
ognition of our inability to see into the future has given rise
to better techniques within the trust formula for carrying out
the intentions of the grantor.

One method of allowing for the unexpected is to give the trustees discretion in distributing income. The trust instrument may provide that the trustees can distribute income among a group of beneficiaries in varying proportions, depending on the circumstances at the time. The most obvious need for such a provision is in a trust for minors. The amount of money needed for the support of a minor varies greatly as he develops through the years. Usually, the decision of how much and to whom income should be distributed each year can be made best as events unfold. The grantor may specify in the instrument the criteria to be used by the trustees in making distributions, or he may have sufficient confidence in the trustees to follow the often used course of allowing them complete discretion. This same type of discretion can be granted the trustees with respect to making distributions out of the trust principal as the need arises. Often the grantor will want the trustees to be able to distribute principal to one or more beneficiaries if circumstances should indicate a need. This can be arranged in the trust instrument. The grantor can set the guidelines for such an occurrence or he can leave it to the judgment of the trustees.

Heavy, graduated income and estate taxes have been largely responsible for the enormous increase in the use of trusts even for moderate estates in the past two decades. The wise use of trusts can result in substantial savings in income and estate taxes. Happily for some, the program of trust planning which should be adopted anyway for family reasons, even without considering tax benefits, is also the program which produces tax savings. For others, compromises may be necessary in weighing nontax objectives with tax-saving techniques.

Most irrevocable trusts fall into the category usually called the *long-term trust*. There is also the *short-term trust*, which has been conceived almost entirely as a creature of the graduated income tax laws, and which is also a form of irrevocable trust.

Long-Term Trusts

Most irrevocable long-term trusts are created by will, but sometimes it is desirable to create an irrevocable trust in connection with the making of a gift during the life of the grantor. Such a gift, if the trust is properly drawn, will remove the property from the grantor's taxable estate for federal estate tax purposes and thus effect the same tax savings as outright gifts. (There may or may not be a gift tax, depending on prior gifts and the size of the trust. But gift taxes are usually far less than estate taxes.) Of course, the problem of gifts in contemplation of death is always present. But if the grantor survives the gift-giving by three years, that problem is eliminated. The grantor is not permitted to reserve any right to receive income or principal from the trust, or the property will be included in his taxable estate in spite of the trust gift. Furthermore, if the grantor retains any substantial administrative power over the trust, either as a co-trustee or otherwise, he runs the risk of losing the estate tax savings. The safest course from a tax standpoint is for the grantor to rely entirely on independent trustees and retain no administrative power over the trust for himself.

An estate tax saving more often related to the trust device is the avoidance of estate taxes in the estate of the trust beneficiary. If a husband dies leaving his property outright to his wife, that property will incur an estate tax at the wife's death. By creating a trust for his wife's benefit, he can eliminate this tax. The wife may still have the absolute right to the income, and distributions of principal to her in event of need may be made in the discretion of the trustee. The same arrangement can be made for other beneficiaries.

Broad flexibility is available with respect to distributions of principal. The beneficiary can even be given a noncumulative right to demand and receive each year a distribution of up to $5,000 or 5% of the trust assets, whichever is greater, without substantially jeopardizing the ultimate tax savings. In addition to distributions which a beneficiary can demand, the trustee can be permitted to distribute substantial amounts of principal to or for the benefit of a beneficiary without upsetting the tax savings. A standard can be set for determining such principal distributions, or complete discretion can be left to the trustee. In short, the law allows the estate planner plenty of room to tailor the trust to meet the individual needs and desires of a particular grantor without endangering the tax savings. This type of planning can be effected for any person the grantor may wish to benefit.

Another type of tax savings from the use of trusts is the income tax savings afforded by *sprinkling trusts*. The sprinkling trust is the trust under which independent trustees are given broad discretion in the distribution of income among beneficiaries.

Because of the graduated income tax rates, a given amount of income will incur the least amount of tax if it is spread among a number of taxpayers, particularly those in a low income tax bracket. As a consequence, the trust may provide that the trustee is to pay the net income from the trust to or for the benefit of the grantor's wife and children, in such proportions and in such manner as the trustees, in their discretion, shall deem necessary or desirable to insure their comfortable care, support, maintenance, education and general welfare. In addition, the trustees may be authorized, in their discretion, to pay at any time any portion of the trust principal to or for the benefit of the grantor's wife or any of his children, whenever in the trustees' opinion the trust income is inadequate to achieve the objectives of the trust. The trustees might be directed to take into account the respective ages, health, educational requirements, earning capacity and other circumstances affecting each beneficiary. The result of such provisions in a trust instrument is to enable the trustees to take care of the financial needs of the various beneficiaries of the trust; at the same time, substantial income tax savings are often achieved because the income from the trust will be taxed to those beneficiaries who actually receive it. If, for example, the grantor's wife has substantial income of her own and is in a high tax bracket, the trustees can direct the income of the trust to the grantor's children who have less income and are in lower income tax brackets. The important thing is that the income can be divided among the beneficiaries of the trust so as to provide maximum tax advantages while still taking care of their needs.

Short-Term Trusts

Our high, graduated income tax rates have given rise to a specialized type of short-term trust designed primarily to shift the income tax burden to a lower tax bracket. This trust is sometimes called the *Clifford Trust*, after a famous court case involving trusts of this type.

A not unusual example is that of a businessman whose income falls into the 50% (or higher) income tax bracket. He is supporting his elderly, widowed mother, who lives modestly and comfortably on $3,000 per year. In order to provide that $3,000 per year after taxes of 50%, the executive must produce at least $6,000 in income. If he could put property into trust for his mother so that the income would directly to her and would be taxed in her own low income tax bracket instead of his, the saving would be startling. By shifting about $3,200 of taxable income to her, he could provide the needed after-tax income of $3,200. Thus he accomplishes, with $3,200 of income from the trust, what before had required $6,000 of his income.

Happily, the tax law does allow this type of savings if the rules are followed carefully. The first essential is that an irrevocable trust be created. Its duration must be at least 10 years if the property is to come back to the grantor at its termination. But it can be made to terminate at the death of the income beneficiary (the mother in our example), if that is desirable, even if she dies before the end of the 10-year period and regardless of her life expectancy.

Since this type of short-term trust is generally not aimed at saving estate taxes, considerably more power can be retained by the grantor than with the long-term irrevocable trust. He can even be the trustee if the trust is drawn so as to prohibit his exercising certain powers, generally related to distribution of income and principal of the trust. There is an exception. If the beneficiary of the trust is a dependent of the grantor, the grantor can reserve the right to determine how much of the income will be distributed to the beneficiary from time to time, so long as any undistributed income is allowed to accumulate in the trust, to be distributed only to the beneficiary (or to his estate if his death terminates the trust) when the trust terminates. But since early 1970, the tax laws have made accumulations of income frequently undesirable.

The support of an elderly dependent mother is only one example of the many uses of this type of trust for a grantor in a high income tax bracket. Children, grandchildren, other relatives and even nonrelatives may be beneficiaries. If minor children are beneficiaries of a trust, care must be taken to assure that the income is not used to satisfy the parent's legal obligation to support the minor children. Any trust income so used may be taxed to the grantor.

Finally, it should be pointed out that a grantor need not be in a tremendously high income tax bracket to find this short-term trust device attractive. Many such trusts now in operation are providing substantial tax savings for taxpayers whose top income tax bracket is less than 50%.

In making the final decision, due account should be taken of the fact that trustees must be paid commissions for administering the trusts. Also (in calculating the net savings that are to be expected) it should not be overlooked that the tax effect of capital gains and losses remains the responsibility of the grantor.

In the case of a Clifford Trust the grantor has made a gift of income. Accordingly, depending on the prior gift on the grantor and the size of this gift as determined by calculations from valuation tables, it is possible that a gift tax return must be filed and gift tax paid.

Summary

Irrevocable trusts, created either during life or by will, are extremely useful estate planning tools, both for tax and non-tax reasons, but the creation of an irrevocable trust during life should be approached with a great deal of caution. Large savings of both estate taxes and income taxes can be realized, while at the same time proper management of property and provisions for effective security for one's family can be assured. But these savings must always be weighed against the fees and expenses of the trust.

17

My Business or Farm

Many people have devoted their lives and energies to developing a successful business enterprise. This business operation may be a sole proprietorship, a partnership or a closely held corporation, and it may involve anything from farming to manufacturing. It may employ two persons or 2,000. Whether the business can survive the death of the individual who was dominant in its development will depend largely on the amount of planning that has been done prior to that individual's death. Unfortunately, many businessmen are so preoccupied with daily business problems that they fail to make proper preparations during their lifetimes for the orderly continuation or disposition of the business after their deaths.

Form of Enterprise

A business may be a sole proprietorship, a partnership or a corporation. In a sole proprietorship the assets of the business are owned by an individual, and upon his death his personal representative has a duty to liquidate or sell the business, unless the will authorizes him to continue its operation.

A partnership is usually dissolved on the death of a partner, and the surviving partners are required by law to liquidate the business and make an accounting to the deceased partner's estate. However, the partnership agreement can provide for continuation of the business or partnership after the death of a partner.

If the business is in corporate form, ownership and control result from ownership of the corporation's stock. Normally, the death of a stockholder (even one owning all of the stock) will have no legal effect on the life of the corporation.

Sale or Continuation

Any business, regardless of its legal form, can become paralyzed following the death of its owner. Uninterrupted production or sales during this period is usually difficult because the individual who has been responsible for the daily operations and decisions is gone. An orderly plan for the transfer of operational and managerial control, or for immediate sale, is essential to insure the realization of maximum values for the owner's family.

The most important decision to be made regarding the business is whether it is to be sold or its operations continued. This decision depends upon a number of factors.

If the owner's personal services were the primary income producing factor, it is probably advisable to sell the business after his death, but if the owner's capital was his principal contribution, it may be in the best interests of the family to arrange for a continuation of the business. The need for cash by the estate and the family, the availability of liquid assets and the projected cash flow of the business are important considerations in the decision as to sale or continuation. The needs and rights of other partners or stockholders must also be considered. Such rights can arise through agreements made with the decedent during his lifetime or they may, as in the case of a partnership, result from operation of law.

Buy-Sell Agreements

Instead of waiting until after the business owner's death to decide upon the sale or continuation of the business, it is much better if this decision is made during the owner's lifetime by means of a buy-sell agreement. Not only is the decision made during a period of comparative calm, rather than in one of anxiety and tension, but it is made by those most familiar with the business, and its implementation is usually provided for in the agreement. In contrast, when a decision is made after death to sell the business, the personal representative is faced with the task of finding a buyer. This is often a difficult if not impossible job.

The buy-sell agreement can be used with any form of business entity but is more common in the partnership or corporation than in the sole proprietorship.

These agreements are not found in a do-it-yourself handbook, but must be tailored to meet the particular situation. Some are binding upon purchaser and seller, while others are merely options or "first refusal" agreements. Funding is often provided through life insurance; payments can be made in full upon death, or provided for in installments; the price may be fixed in dollars or based on a forumla, or may be made contingent, for example, on earnings. The provisions may be as broad and varied as the imagination of the planner and the skill of the draftsman, but they should have two major purposes—to preserve the value of the business for the owner's family and to meet the needs of those who are buying the business. In order to accomplish these objectives, the draftsman must be familiar with various provisions of the federal income, estate and gift tax laws and the Maryland inheritance and estate tax laws.

Powers of the Personal Representative

Where a business represents a substantial portion of the decedent's estate, it is important that his will give the personal representative broad discretionary powers to deal with the problems that may arise. Among these are the powers to continue an unincorporated business, to incorporate it, to sell some or all of the assets, to borrow money, to employ or retain workers, managers and professionals, etc. In short, the personal representative must have sufficient authority to permit prompt action and to exercise sound business judgment.

Liquidity

Death creates a need for cash. Funds must be provided for the family's living expenses, for taxes, for the decedent's debts and often for the business itself.

If the business or its assets are to be sold, the terms of the sale should be framed to insure the availability of funds for these needs. If the business is to be continued after death, the owner's estate and business planning must provide the funds necessary to pay the various taxes involved.

In a sole proprietorship this may be accomplished by providing life insurance for the estate, by providing for the sale of specific assets for cash, or by providing the personal representative with appropriate directions and powers to borrow the necessary funds.

In a partnership agreement provisions for funds to pay taxes may be made by providing for withdrawals from the deceased partner's capital account. Current partnership earnings can also be used for this purpose for a period after death. Other alternatives here, too, are life insurance, the sale of assets and borrowing.

The owners of a closely held corporation will likely experience great difficulty in raising cash through the sale of corporate stock, due to the limited market for these securities. However, under certain conditions the law permits the corporation to redeem some of the stock in order to pay funeral expenses, death taxes and other costs involved in administering the decedent's estate. This means that the corporate business can be used to provide the cash funds needed without any adverse tax consequences. This privilege of stock redemption is one that should be carefully studied in the estate plan, as it provides many opportunities for preserving the value of a corporate business.

Summary

There are no cure-all substitutes for thorough business planning to preserve the value of a business at the time of the owner's death. Nor is there a device by which all problems created at death can be easily resolved.

A well-considered plan, designed to cover the particular problems of the business and to meet the needs and goals of the individual and his family, is essential to preserve and protect the value of the business at the owner's death.

Experience shows that the purchase of life insurance on the various owners is the best possible way to provide for liquidity for buy-out by a surviving partner, for buy-out by the corporation (a very important and—if properly planned—valuable tax-saving tool) or for buy-out by surviving stockholders. Space only permits reference here to this most valuable estate planning vehicle, but the reader can be assured that the lawyer who plans a will normally advises his client of the absolute necessity of considering life insurance for these purposes.

18

Powers of Attorney

In Maryland the law with respect to powers of attorney and their duration is dramatically different from the law that exists in most other states and from the law that existed in Maryland up until 1969.

The traditional common law rule was that a power of attorney, by which someone appoints another to take care of one or more of his affairs, would become ineffective upon the occurrence of a disability. That meant that if the person who granted the power of attorney became seriously ill or disabled, a person holding the power of attorney no longer had the right to use the power. The power of attorney was revoked by the illness just as effectively as though the person had actually withdrawn it or had died.

Under Maryland law as it exists today the draftsman of a power of attorney can use language which will permit a power of attorney to continue to exist during all periods of disability, uninterrupted by the old common law rule.

Most laymen have felt, in the past, that powers of attorney were drafted primarily to take care of people who were disabled. And so they were disconcerted, to say the least, to find, when (for example) a parent became ill, that a bank or a brokerage house which learned about the illness refused to honor the power of attorney. In the view of many lawyers the law was not really carrying out the purpose of individuals who executed powers of attorney, and therefore the Section of Estate and Trust Law of the Maryland State Bar Association recommended in 1969, among other reforms, that the Maryland legislature enact this far-reaching change in the law.

The effect is that where powers of attorney are properly drafted and where a person has enough confidence in the one that he nominates as his attorney-in-fact (the person who holds the power of attorney) to let him manage his affairs during any period of illness or disability, the mechanism now exists to do this with a modicum of trouble and a minimum of expense.

No longer will it be necessary to have a committee or guardian appointed by a court; no longer will it be necessary to set up a living deed of trust simply for the purpose of taking care of a person during disability. There are many other valid reasons for having a deed of trust, but one of them will no longer be that someone might become ill. What now may be done is to have a *current* power of attorney—and this means that if possible it is advisable that one be signed every couple of years—naming a person to act as an attorney-in-fact, and the instrument can also provide that even if a legal guardian must be appointed for any reason, there need not be a bond posted by the guardian. Finally, the power of attorney can also name the person who should be appointed a guardian if for some unexpected reason a guardianship should be necessary.

Thus the law reform movement grows in Maryland. The existence of this new law means that in many cases such a power of attorney, placed in the hands of a qualified person or persons, will fully substitute for the more ponderous and expensive revocable trust (as discussed in Chapter 13).

19

Powers of Appointment

Powers of appointment permit testators to do a great many things which they can accomplish by no other method. Powers of appointment have been referred to as the most efficient device by which a testator may obtain great flexibility in his estate plan while still controlling the general purposes to which his property shall be devoted.

Let us assume that widow Smith has a $200,000 estate. She has been told that if her will leaves her entire estate outright to her son, John, there will be estate taxes both at the time she dies and the time her son dies. Therefore, she decides to leave her estate in trust for the benefit of her son. As indicated in chapters 4 and 16, this trust will not be taxable at the time her son dies, so that one generation of estate taxes will be skipped. This conclusion will follow even though the trustees are to pay all of the income to the son and even though the trustees may have the discretion to invade the principal of the trust for the son in the event of any emergency. Customarily, such a trust provides that when her son dies, the trust will terminate and the trustees will pay the principal of the trust to the son's children living at the time the son dies. The widow Smith, however, says that her son's children are now only 5, 9 and 13 years old, and that by the time her son dies, which may be 40 or 50 years hence, it might not be sensible for the trustees to distribute the trust in equal shares to the three children. One of the children might have become a spendthrift, one of them might have become a multimillionaire, while the other by reason of chronic illness needs substantial funds to pay for medical bills and the necessities of life. The widow Smith realizes that she will not be alive when these children become adults so that she will not be able, in her own will, to determine the most sensible manner of ultimate distribution. She would, however, like to give her son the opportunity to determine the disposition of the trust, but also to avoid having the trust assets included in his gross estate for federal estate tax purposes when he dies. The answer to her problem, of course, is the power of appointment. She will give to her son a power of appointment. This means that her son, by his will, is given the power to appoint—or designate—the ultimate beneficiaries of the trust property. Assuming that the will creating the power of appointment is carefully drafted, the assets subject to the power of appointment will not be taxed in the son's estate.

The power of appointment can be as broad or as narrow as the widow Smith desires. She can provide that her son may appoint (by his will, of course) the property only to his children, or only to his children and grandchildren, or only to his children, his wife, and his grandchildren, or to any one in his family, or to anyone at all in the world. She can also provide that the son may appoint the property by requiring the trust to terminate, or that the son may continue the property in trust after he dies for the benefit of those persons whom he designates in his will. The advantage of the power of appointment is that the son, many years after the widow Smith has died, has had the opportunity to watch his children grow up and to determine whether an equal outright distribution in thirds would be the most desirable or whether some other disposition should be made. The property subject to the power will not be taxable at the son's death whether or not he exercises the power.

Great care must be taken in drafting powers of appointment. In Maryland, which is unique in the United States, a power "to appoint to any one my son desires" does not enable him to appoint the property to his estate or his creditors. Ordinarily, this is of no great moment, because widow Smith would presumably not care if her son had the power to appoint to his estate or to his creditors so long as he can appoint to the members of his family.

The chief problem with respect to powers of appointment in Maryland is their use in connection with marital deduction trusts. As pointed out in Chapter 6, a trust which a husband creates for his wife will qualify for the marital deduction *only* if the wife has a power to appoint to her estate. If the husband merely gives his wife a power "to appoint to any one she desires" under Maryland law, she does not have the power to appoint to her estate and therefore the trust will not qualify for the marital deduction. There have been a number of cases which have arisen with respect to Maryland wills where the draftsmen failed to use the proper terminology in qualifying the trust for the marital deduction. The only way to qualify such a trust for the marital deduction in Maryland is to state in substance that the wife will have the power to appoint the trust to her estate and such other persons as she may desire.

The type of power of appointment used in a marital deduction trust is called a general power of appointment. If the holder of a power has a general power of appointment, the property subject to the power will be included in the gross estate of the holder of the power. For marital deduction purposes, this means that although the trust will not be taxed in the husband's estate when he dies first; rather it will be taxed later in the wife's estate. Where a special power of appointment is given to the holder of a power, the property subject to the power is not subject to federal estate taxes in the estate of the holder of the power, but a special power will not qualify for the marital deduction.

20

Time Schedule for Estate Administration

Frequently, complaints are heard that the administration of an estate in Maryland, either for the probate of a will or in intestacy, is unduly delayed and that too much time elapses before a final accounting is rendered. Actually, the time required for complete settlement of an estate in Maryland has been shortened by recently enacted statutes, and delays are only warranted in unusual cases. There are always some situations, however, in which the provisions of the federal income and estate tax laws might make it advantageous to keep the estate open. For example, under certain circumstances estate taxes may be paid over a 10-year period, or income taxes may be saved by continuing the estate as a taxpayer separate and distinct from the beneficiaries.

On occasion, estates will have extensive real estate holdings or family business interests which cannot be disposed of promptly without considerable loss. Good business judgment on the part of the personal representative may require in these cases that final settlement be postponed to prevent diminution of the assets through forced or hurried sales.

The Personal Representative

In carrying out Maryland probate administration, the personal representative has important duties and obligations, many of which would still be necessary even if a living trust had been created by the decedent.

When a Maryland resident dies, the funeral arrangements are usually made by a member of the immediate family. However, in many instances there are no immediate survivors, or if existing, they are a considerable distance away. In these cases, the personal representative will be expected to carry out the burial instructions of the decedent, to notify family members or friends, and to arrange for the security of property until probate of the will. If there are family members, he meets with them to determine their immediate needs, even before probate, and to assist in preparing insurance claims, notifying employer insurance or benefit funds and contacting the Social Security Administration or other appropriate agencies.

The personal representative must then obtain the will, either from family members, a safe deposit box, or other source of safe-keeping and arrange for its probate. A safe deposit box may be opened, with proper safeguards, to permit a search for a will. The general practice is that the attorney for the estate then offers the will for probate and obtains from the court letters authorizing the personal representative to take his office. At this point, the personal representative begins collecting the assets of the estate. He transfers bank accounts to an estate account or accounts, applies for any insurance payable to the estate as beneficiary, obtains a list of and secures custody of stock certificates, notes, motor vehicle titles and other assets of the estate. Under present Maryland law title to real estate owned individually by the decedent also passes to the personal representative, so that he must determine what realty is

involved, notify tenants or lessees, satisfy himself that
adequate insurance coverage is in effect, or secure the same,
collect rents and provide for payment of taxes, insurance,
utilities and other current expenses. He must get a "tax
number" from the Internal Revenue Service. If there is a
business, provisions must be made for its continued operation, and this may require the employment of someone
qualified to manage the business during the period of
probate.

In securing possession of estate assets the personal
representative must determine whether or not the various
items properly belong in the probate estate or were jointly
held with co-owners who survive or as tenants by the entireties with a surviving spouse. In Maryland property held as
tenancy by the entireties is not a part of the probate estate
and need not be returned in any inventories by the personal
representative; the jointly owned property (including joint
savings accounts) is not included in the estate inventories but
is returned on separate joint tenancy forms (unless owned
with a spouse). One of the personal representative's duties is
to prepare and file these joint tenancy reports and to see that
proper inheritance taxes are paid.

Care must be taken not to include the proceeds of jointly
owned property such as dividends in the estate bank
accounts, and not to mix the assets of the estate with those
of the personal representative.

The personal representative must make the necessary
arrangements for the preparation of inventories. Appraisers
under present Maryland law are often chosen by the personal
representative, who must notify them of the estate assets,
frequently accompany them when the actual inventory is
made, and review the valuation placed on the estate assets.
The old mandatory system of court-appointed appraisers
(with their accompanying fees) has been abolished in
Maryland, and with assets whose value is readily determinable

such as securities listed on stock exchanges and bank accounts the personal representative may appraise them himself.

During administration the personal representative must pay the bills of the estate, including the funeral bill, outstanding accounts at the date of death, current expenses, administration costs and taxes. To meet these expenses the personal representative may be obliged to liquidate stocks or other estate assets. This requires that the personal representative have sufficient business knowledge to make sales in the best interest of the estate.

Among other duties of the personal representative are those of preparing final income tax returns for the decedent and paying any taxes due. Fiduciary income tax returns for the income of the estate must be prepared and the taxes paid by the personal representative. If the gross estate exceeds $60,000 he will have the duty of preparing and filing both federal and Maryland estate tax returns and paying any taxes which result. If these taxes are not paid when due, penalties and interest accrue, so that it is essential that the returns be filed and the taxes paid on time. Under proper circumstances, a personal representative may be required to request a time extension for tax payment to avoid penalties. This will occur most frequently in estates lacking sufficient liquidity.

Detailed records must be kept by the personal representative to preserve the facts as to all receipts and payments. Allocation must be made between items of income and of principal. This information will be necessary to state the various accounts and to prepare the numerous tax returns. Frequently, the best interests of the estate will require the personal representative to dispose of certain assets to prevent loss or diminution of the estate.

When administration is complete, all assets collected and expenses paid, the personal representative must make final distribution. If a will is involved, he must distribute in accordance with its provisions; in cases of intestacy the personal representative distributes in accordance with the Maryland intestacy law. In either case, he should time all distributions to give maximum tax benefits to the beneficiaries. When distribution has been made in accordance with a final administration account, the estate is terminated.

Time Sequence of Administration

Proving the Will

With the above very brief outline of the duties of a personal representative in mind, it is easier to understand the sequence of steps in probate. Generally, the family will attempt immediately after death to locate the will to determine if the will contains any funeral instructions. If there is no immediate family, the personal representative may already have the will and be aware of the instructions. If such instructions exist, they should of course be complied with. There is no specific statute in Maryland setting forth the time within which a will must be probated or an estate opened, but practical considerations generally dictate that there be prompt probate. There usually are motor vehicles to be transferred, a business to operate, rents to collect, bills to be paid, or other items demanding prompt attention. For example, it is necessary to obtain immediately proper endorsements and limits of liability and to review the entire insurance situation.

The personal representative must secure a list of names and addresses of all persons named in the will, and of all persons who would be heirs if the decedent died without a will. In most cases this is not difficult, but problems are occasionally presented when the next-of-kin are nephews or nieces, or their descendants, or cousins. Within 20 days of appointment, the personal representative must deliver to the Register of Wills a copy of the published newspaper notice of his appointment and the list of legatees and heirs. The Register of Wills then forwards a copy of the newspaper notice to each heir or legatee within five days of receiving it from the personal representative.

No preliminary notice is required before probate. The personal representative files an application for letters of administration and offers the will. If the petition shows that the decedent was a resident of Maryland and of the city or county in which application is made and the will appears to have been properly executed, letters of administration are granted. Unless there is to be an objection, Maryland law does not require the personal appearance in court of anyone, even the personal representative. The personal representative must file the required bond and accept the appointment as personal representative before actual receipt of the certificate which proves his appointment. When this has been done the estate is open, the personal representative has qualified and administration begins.

In the average case this point is reached within two or three weeks after death, but this depends on how rapidly the family obtains the required information and how soon application for letters of administration is filed.

Collecting and Valuing Property

Immediately after qualifying, the personal representative begins the process of collecting and identifying the assets. The time involved here depends on the nature and complexity of the estate. If there are few assets and no claims of consequence, the process of identifying the assets is simple. The assets must, however, be evaluated for tax purposes, and that may or may not consume an appreciable amount of time, depending on the kind and quantity of the assets involved and whether an expert appraisal is found to be necessary. If there is tangible personal property such as jewelry, antiques or paintings which have substantial value, it is customary to obtain an expert appraisal and to furnish a copy of this with the inventory. These appraisals are usually done rapidly by professionals. Real estate appraisals, on the other hand, generally take longer. If the value of the real estate is very substantial as well as very doubtful, the personal representative may wish to obtain more than one expert appraisal so as to be prepared if the tax auditors disagree about the reported value.

An understanding of the process of real estate appraisal also aids an understanding of the time requirements. Property in the same general location and category will have generally the same characteristics. Information covering recent sales of property in the same general location and category should be obtained in order for the appraiser to determine value. It takes time for real estate information to be assembled, sorted and evaluated. If the property is to be sold shortly after death, the sales price is usually a reliable figure. If, however, no sale of the property is contemplated, to establish the fair market value of that property it is necessary to determine the answer to a hypothetical question: What would a willing buyer be willing to pay a seller who is willing to sell on the date of the decedent's death? While this is a matter of opinion, there must be some rational basis for determining the answer which can be documented and made part of the appraisal.

Another kind of property which requires time to value is closely held stock. If the stock in the estate is a listed stock on which market quotations appear daily, the matter of valuation is simple. However, a family corporation in which there may not have been a sale of stock for many years and where sales that have occurred may not be representative due to special circumstances presents a much more complex, time-consuming problem.

Much time could be saved for the personal representative by a careful planning of this valuation process by the testator. If he leaves a detailed list of assets accompanied by much of the necessary data for appraisal purposes, the job of the personal representative will be simplified and shortened. If he has entered into a proper "buy-sell" agreement during his lifetime, the value fixed in that agreement will be binding. (See Chapter 17.)

Time for Filing Creditors' Claims

Under present Maryland statutes, the claims of creditors must be filed within six months after the date of the first appointment of the personal representative.

As a practical matter, personal representatives generally do not require formal filing of claims for small items such as utility bills, small accounts and other claims when there is no question as to their propriety.

To protect himself, the personal representative may decide not to pay claims until the filing period (six months) has passed, in order to determine accurately the solvency of the estate. Where solvency is not in doubt, there is normally no reason to delay payment of undisputed bills. No final accounting and distribution can be filed until this six-month period has elapsed, but reasonably soon thereafter the personal representative should pay any remaining valid and undisputed claims.

The personal representative may, therefore, take a reasonable time to pay the claims of the estate. If the claims are few and uncomplicated, payment can be made rapidly and the estate readied for distribution to the beneficiaries. If litigation arises, if there are large numbers of claims, or if the validity of some claims is shrouded in dispute, the personal representative has adequate opportunity to dispose of these matters in the sensible, normal way that the testator could have done had he lived.

Accounting and Distribution

When provision has been made for the payment of all debts and taxes, the personal representative is ready to make distribution. Maryland law requires a first accounting to be filed within nine months after giving notice of the appointment of the personal representative, with subsequent accounts to be filed each six months. Unless there are undetermined tax liabilities or pending litigation involving the estate, the initial account can actually be the final account in many small estates. Notice of the filing of any account must be given to all interested parties within the 15-day period preceding the filing. Before the account is approved, inheritance tax is due on any legacy being paid. Also, the tax on the commissions of the personal representative, described in Chapter 5, must be paid when the account is approved.

The Impact of Taxes

Federal Estate Tax

Formerly, the federal tax law requirements often caused longer delays in settling estate because the federal estate tax return was due 15 months after the date of death. Now, however, in the case of decedents dying on and after January 1, 1971, the federal estate tax return is due and the tax must be paid (except in unusual instances which need not be discussed here) nine months after the date of death.

The federal estate tax law permits the estate to be valued as of the date of death, or as of a date six months after death. The personal representative has the option of using the lower of these two valuations, so that it is frequently necessary to re-appraise estate assets as of the later date. This should not involve much additional time or expense, as the basic work of appraisal was completed at the date of death appraisal. There is no benefit to be gained by advance payment of the federal estate tax, so that it is usually paid near the end of the nine-month period. This period will tie in with the due date of the first account in the Maryland probate proceeding, so that in most cases the first accounting in Maryland may include the federal estate tax paid.

Income tax

The federal income tax sometimes prompts a longer extension of the administration period. Income tax brackets rise even more sharply than estate tax brackets. For federal income tax purposes, the estate—which comes into being at the moment of death—is a separate taxpayer with a separate exemption and a separate applicable tax bracket. During the period that the estate remains open, it provides a separate pocket into which income may be placed and on which federal income tax may be payable at a lower rate than for either the decedent or the beneficiary. If the tax bracket applicable to the beneficiaries is higher than that applicable to the estate, it will benefit the beneficiaries to maintain the estate as a taxpayer for as long as permissible under federal law.

It is probable that estates which remain open from two to five years or more are kept open mainly for federal tax reasons rather than delinquency or mismanagement on the part of lawyers, judges, personal representatives or appraisers. The simple truth is that a personal representative who does his job thoroughly will not close the estate so long as it is in the best interest of the beneficiaries to keep it open, assuming of course that he operates within the rules laid down by the Internal Revenue Service and by the courts. Planning by the testator and subsequently by the personal representative can indicate to what extent keeping the estate open for a substantial period is of advantage to the beneficiaries.

In the final analysis, if a proper will is drawn naming a competent personal representative, the paper work steps will not be the time-consuming factor. The real delay will be caused by the intricacies of the federal tax laws and by the heavy burden of federal estate and income taxes.

State Inheritance and Estate Taxes

At the time of distribution, the state inheritance tax must be paid. This tax is more fully explained in Chapter 5. There is no discount for advance payment, but interest becomes due and payable at 1/2% per month on inheritance taxes not paid within 30 days after the due date.

Also, the Maryland estate tax return is due and payable 15 months after the date of death. This tax consists of only the credit due on the federal return for state taxes and does not result in any additional tax burden on the estate. The return is filed with the Register of Wills in the city or county of administration, but the tax is paid directly to the Comptroller of Treasury.

Comparison with the Living Trust

The living trust may simplify the problem of passing on certain assets. On the other hand, there will be little or no time saved at death so far as ultimate settlement of the estate is concerned. The assets of that trust must be listed and valued for federal estate and Maryland inheritance tax purposes. The same valuation and tax procedures must be followed as if the trust had not been created. The personal representative must take care of all assets not in the trust, and all other procedures regarding those assets must be followed. It makes little difference so far as the time factor is concerned that trust assets may not appear as part of the probate inventory. The commissions for personal representatives are of course lower, but the overall cost may or may not be lower depending on all the facts.

The living trust can actually result in increased expense. In one respect, the living trust is definitely disadvantageous in that it prevents the personal representative from utilizing the estate as a separate federal income tax-lowering pocket. The trust does not ordinarily receive the favorable treatment which the estate, as a separate tax pocket, enjoys under the federal tax laws. Even though the estate is not within the federal estate tax bracket, the income tax savings by reason of the estate's separate taxpayer status may well justify passing of income from estate to trust or beneficiary. The amounts saved in any one year are not large in themselves, but they can be very substantial when projected over the period of estate administration. In a large estate, the presence of this extra tax pocket during the estate administration may make the probate procedures worth the choice of this route over the revocable trust.

Estate administration through probate is not significantly more time consuming than through a living trust. A living trust for all of the decedent's property has its uses, but its virtues are often outweighed by the loss of important tax advantages if the estate is passed in full or in part through administration by a capable personal representative.

Summary

In general, it is probable that most small estates in Maryland—i.e., those not requiring federal estate tax returns—can be closed within a year after administration is begun. In many instances the first account, required after nine months, can also serve as the final account. Most other estates can be completed by the time another account is required in an additional six months. The unusual estate involving complicated business operations, federal estate tax problems, or liquidations may take considerably longer, but these represent a small percentage of the estates administered in Maryland.

21

What Will Probate Cost?

Of universal interest is the question, "What will probate cost my estate?" The answer involves careful consideration of the size, type and location of the present and future assets comprising the estate, any tax complications, the simplicity or complexity of the disposition of the estate, the extent and type of the debts and various other factors.

This chapter will deal with costs and expenses in relatively routine administrations. It will not cover probate intricacies in unusual situations, will contests, complicated probate litigation, or appeals from actions taken by the probate courts, since such matters are not usually present and therefore are outside the scope of this book.

Apart from estate and inheritance taxes, the two larger costs of probate are likely to be the commissions of the personal representatives and attorneys' fees. These commissions and fees represent compensation to those who do the real work of handling the administration of an estate. Actually, it is not entirely fair to consider the commissions of personal representatives and fees of attorneys as expenses of *probate*. They are really expenses which result from the work—primarily the tax problems—brought about by someone dying and the necessity for someone else to provide for the orderly transmissions of property interests to survivors, and the reporting and payment of taxes, whether or not there is probate. In other words, many of the same essential duties will be required of someone who survives the decedent, whether such survivor be family, friend, lawyer, trust company or someone else, regardless of whether the decedent's property passes by probate or by some other method of disposition. Someone will have to gather information for the decedent's final United States and State of Maryland income tax returns and, thereafter, prepare and file the returns. Someone will have to prepare and file a federal estate tax return, a Maryland estate tax return and the material for Maryland inheritance taxes and pay all taxes due. Someone will have to apply for and collect the decedent's life insurance proceeds, apply for Social Security benefits, arrange for payment of funeral and burial expenses, arrange for transfer of title to all real estate owned by the decedent as well as his motor vehicles, boats, securities, bank accounts, etc., even though they may be jointly owned, to mention only a few of the very numerous duties that are always left for someone to perform when someone else dies. Of course, when there is probate these duties are performed as directed by the personal representatives and their attorneys.

Commissions of Personal Representatives

In the State of Maryland, the commissions (fees) of the personal representatives are fixed by the Orphans' Court (in Montgomery County, the Circuit Court sitting as an Orphans' Court) in the county where the estate is being administered. Unless the will provides a larger measure of compensation, the commissions of the personal representatives may not exceed the limits set by statutory provision. The top limits provided by the Maryland Code, Article 93, Section 7-601, are as follows:

If the property subject to administration is	The commissions shall not exceed
Not over $20,000	10% thereof
Over $20,000.	$2,000 plus 4% of the excess over $20,000

No commissions are allowed on real property or the income from it. When, however, any real property is sold by the personal representative, the Orphans' Court is authorized by statute to allow commissions on such sale, not to exceed 10% of the proceeds. As a practical matter, the courts usually take into consideration any real estate brokers' commissions paid in effectuating such sales and allow the personal representatives commissions at the rate of 10% of the sales proceeds, reduced, however, by any amounts paid to real estate brokers.

The statutory amounts are the maximum allowed by the Orphans' Court as commissions to personal representatives and may not be exceeded. They apply regardless of the number of personal representatives—there may be one, two, three, four or more. Only one commission within the statutory limits will be allowed. This does not mean, however, that the Orphans' Court will automatically allow the maximum commissions provided for by statute. On the contrary, the Maryland probate law requires a personal representative applying for commissions to petition for the commissions, setting forth in reasonable detail in his petition the nature of the services rendered to the estate entitling him to a commission. Notice of such a petition must be served upon all persons interested in the decedent's estate, and such persons are then given an opportunity to be heard in opposition to the allowance of the commissions for which the personal representative has petitioned.

Maryland has a unique taxing provision known as a tax on commissions of personal representatives. The tax is based on the amount of the commissions allowed or on a statutory formula, whichever provides a larger tax. Thus, the tax on commissions is either 10% of the commissions allowed, or 1% on the first $20,000 of the estate's personal assets (fee simple property is excluded) plus 0.20% on the balance, whichever is larger. This has the effect of requiring a tax to be paid even in cases where the personal representative does not request any commissions, but waives them. Where the personal representative does take commissions, the tax is deducted from the amount of the personal representative's commissions. As a result, the net commissions which the personal representative actually receives are necessarily always less than the maximum commissions which the Orphans' Court, by statute, may allow. Of course, where the personal representative waives commissions, the tax definitely appears as one of the costs of probate.

Attorneys' Fees

With the exception of his own attorney's fee, the lawyer for the estate can usually make a fairly close estimate of most of the costs of probate by the time the value of the estate's assets becomes pretty well known. Since, however, the amount of the attorney's fee is based primarily on the amount of work which he may be required to do, an accurate estimate of such fees, in probate matters, as in other legal matters, may have to await further developments during the course of administration. Usually, by the time the federal estate tax return has been prepared (where such a return is required by law), the work required by the attorney is evident and the fees may then be determined with reasonable accuracy.

Unlike the case of commissions of personal representatives, Maryland statute does not set a maximum rate schedule for attorneys' fees. Here again, however, the amount of attorneys' fees is subject to allowance by the court. Accordingly, both the beneficiaries of the estate and the attorneys

for the estate have a measure of protection through the
supervision exercised by the applicable court of probate. The
Maryland Code, Article 93, Section 7-602 provides:

> Upon the filing of a petition in reasonable detail by the personal
> representative, or by the attorney, the court may allow a counsel fee
> to the attorney employed by the personal representative for legal
> services, which compensation shall be fair and reasonable in the light
> of all the circumstances to be considered in fixing the same.
>
> *Considered with commissions*—If the court shall allow a counsel fee
> to one or more attorneys it shall take into consideration, in making
> such determination, what would be a fair and reasonable total charge
> for the cost of administering the estate * * *, and it shall not allow
> aggregate compensation in excess of that figure.

The Maryland State Bar Association has adopted a
Statewide Suggested Minimum Fee Schedule applicable to
estate administration. It is important to remember, however,
in reviewing this schedule, that it is a suggested schedule of
minimum fees (as contrasted with the Maryland statute providing for commissions of personal representatives, which sets
the *maximum* rates). The provisions of the schedule follow:

> In the administration of a decedent's estate there are actually two
> types of services to be performed, to wit, (a) the non-legal adminis-
> tration services which are often assigned by the testator to a lay
> executor, and (b) the activities and decisions of a legal nature related
> thereto which are traditionally performed by "the lawyer for the
> estate." The distinction between the two in the course of an adminis-
> tration is often difficult to preserve. And this is particularly true
> since (except where a professional executor is used) the lawyer is
> frequently called on to perform a great deal of the non-legal, or
> purely administrative, work.
>
> In earlier days, when estates were less complicated and tax problems
> were relatively insignificant, the "administrative services" represented
> the major portion of the work, with the legal services being relatively

unimportant. Today, in view of the complex nature of many forms of property rights, and in view of the ever increasing importance of post mortem estate and tax planning, these positions have actually become reversed.

In addition, estates which differ in size and composition may differ even to a greater extent in the administration, as well as legal, attention that is required for the proper and complete disposition of each individual's assets, whether according to specific testamentary instructions, or by intestacy, or under non-probate arrangements of various sorts.

With the above as a guide, it is suggested that the duties of lawyers in the settlement of estates be classified into three categories, one as the absolute minimum type of case, with no complications, the next as the normal case, and the third as the extraordinary one.

But, in each case it is essential also to remember that Canon 12 of the Canons of Professional Ethics of the American Bar Association should always be carefully weighed in establishing the ultimate charge for the lawyer.

(1) For the simple estate, where the administration is uncomplicated and easily performed with a minimum of effort, so that the allowance for executor's commissions should also be at a minimum figure, the following amounts are recommended as fair and reasonable minimum fees:

Estates of up to $5,000	up to $150
Estates of $5,000 to $15,000	$250
Estates of $15,000 to $60,000	$500
Estates of $60,000 to $120,000	$1,000
Estates in excess of $120,000	$1,500

The substantial increase for estates in excess of $60,000 is to reflect the added work and responsibility in connection with the requisite estate tax returns, plus the usually more complicated income tax returns (for decedent and estate) at this level, and all decisions to be made in connection therewith (e.g., as to how to take deductions).

(2) As a guideline for the "normal" estate, that is where the work required is more than the minimum effort for the estates described in (1) because the assets constituting the decedent's gross estate, and the work required in the administration thereof, relating both to probate and non-probate assets, might be called the "normal" estate, with the "normal" legal problems:

Based on the maximum allowance of executor's commission, after deducting therefrom the State tax on executor's commissions, an amount equal to—

> For probate estate up to $250,000 ... 1/2 of such executor's commissions
>
> For probate estate in excess of $250,000 ... 1/2 of such executor's commissions for the first $250,000 and 1/4 of such executor's commissions for the amount in excess of $250,000.

(3) Additional compensation, over and above that recommended in either (1) or (2), should be considered fair and reasonable where the attorney is called upon for "unusual services" during the administration of the estate, such "unusual services" to include, but not be limited to—

> (i) representation of the estate in the prosecution or the defense of an action at law or in equity, or in a proceeding before an administrative body;
>
> (ii) services rendered in connection with any asset owned by the decedent or taxed in his eatate, which is not included in any inventory of the personal estate; and
>
> (iii) extraordinary services rendered in connection with the valuation of any asset for tax purposes, or in connection with the audit of estate or inheritance tax returns.

Canon 12 of the Canons of Professional Ethics has been replaced by Disciplinary Rules of a new Code of Professional Responsibility. This new Code states that the following factors should be considered as guidelines in determining the reasonableness of a fee: (1) the time and labor required, the novelty and difficulty of the questions involved, and the skill requisite to perform the legal service properly; (2) the fee customarily charged in the locality for similar legal services; (3) the amount involved and the results obtained; (4) the time limitations imposed by the client or by the circumstances; (5) the nature and length of the professional relationship with the client; (6) the experience, reputation and ability of the lawyer or lawyers performing the services; and (7) the likelihood, if apparent to the client, that the acceptance of the particular employment will preclude other employment by the lawyer.

As is the case in connection with the allowance of commissions of personal representatives, attorneys' fees in Maryland are allowed by the courts only after written notice of the proposed fee, setting forth "in reasonable detail the amount to be requested and the basis therefor" has been given to all interested persons. This procedure affords the beneficiaries of the estate an opportunity to ask the Orphans' Court for a hearing on the commissions and on the attorneys' fees to be allowed, thus giving them the opportunity in all cases of requesting a hearing on these important aspects of estate settlement. Where the lawyer also serves as the personal representative or where there is a personal representative (such as a widow) who expects the lawyer to do most of the work of settling the estate, the fees are frequently far less than the charges where there are separate commissions paid to the non-lawyer personal representative.

Bond Premiums

Another cost of probate to be considered is the premium on the personal representative's bond for the faithful performance of his duties. Maryland law requires that every personal representative shall execute a bond to the State of Maryland for the benefit of all interested persons and creditors, with a surety or sureties approved by the Register of Wills for the county where the estate is administered, unless such bond is expressly excused by the decedent's will or by the written waiver of all interested persons. The penalty of such bond is usually in an amount which equals the probable maximum value of the estate. Where, however, the personal representative is excused from bond, the Register of Wills or the Orphans' Court will, nevertheless, still require a bond in an amount sufficient to secure the payment of (1) debts, (2) Maryland inheritances taxes and (3) Maryland taxes on commissions of the personal representative; such a bond is called a nominal bond.

The premiums on bonds of fiduciaries are standard and as approved by the State Insurance Commissioner. The minimum annual premium is $10.00 for a bond in the penalty of $1,000 or less. The rates per $1,000 are as follows:

	Per $1,000
Up to $2,000	$10.00
$2,000 to $50,000	5.00
$50,000 to $200,000	4.00
$200,000 to $500,000	3.00
$500,000 to $1,500,000	2.00
Over $1,500,000	1.00

Using the above rates, therefore, and assuming an estate of $200,000, all distributable to the children of the decedent, it will be seen that the Register of Wills or Orphans' Court might require a $200,000 bond which would result in the estate's paying an annual premium of $860. If, however, the decedent by his will excused his personal representative from giving bond, the nominal bond of $3,000 which would be required would cost the estate only $25 for the annual premium. Thus, in such a case a well-drawn will might save the estate $835 in probate costs.

In Maryland, fiduciary bonds are not required from banks and trust companies when they serve in the capacity of personal representatives. In addition, an individual serving as a co-fiduciary with a bank or trust company is entitled to a 33 1/3% discount on his bond premium (but not below the minimum of $10). While, usually, the surety on the personal representative's bond is a corporation authorized to act as such in the State of Maryland, the Register of Wills may accept one or more individuals as sureties. In addition, the personal representative's bond—and, therefore, the annual premium on the bond—may be reduced if the personal representative will post collateral with the court or will deposit any cash included in the estate's assets with a banking institution approved by the court in an account expressly made subject to withdrawal only in such manner as the court shall approve.

Charges of the Register of Wills

Maryland provides by statute (Article 36, Section 24) for the fees and charges which may be made by the Register of Wills, and these, of course, are part of the cost of probate. The fees and charges are listed, item by item, in the statute, and only a few examples need be mentioned here.

The charge for taking probate of wills and issuing letters of administration in connection with the usual administration of an estate (called administrative probate) is $7.50. For entering on the estate docket (required for all estates) all papers filed, so that the docket will show a complete list of all incidents connected with the administration of estates, the charge is $3.50. For filing a renunciation of heirs or legatees, personal representatives, guardians, trustees, etc., the charge is $0.75. Each certificate of letters of administration will cost $0.75. For filing and recording wills, inventories, accounts of sales, releases, guardian accounts, administration accounts, petitions and orders, and any other paper to be filed or recorded, the charge is $1.50 per page if double-spaced on typewriter and $3.00 per page, if single-spaced.

From these representative examples of charges of the Register of Wills it is apparent that the Register's charges are not at all substantial. As may be expected, of course, larger and more complicated estates, with more papers to be filed over a longer period of time, will have proportionately greater charges to pay the Register of Wills. A realistic comprehension of charges made by the Register of Wills can be gained by referring to a few typical estates recently administered in the Orphans' Courts of Baltimore City and Baltimore County. In one estate amounting to $7,000, the Register's charges were $30.75. Another estate, with total assets of $10,000, paid the Register of Wills' charges of $69.95. In a $60,000 estate, the Register's charges were $111.00. An estate of $115,000 had Register of Wills' charges amounting to $282.75, while one with assets of $150,000 had charges of $155.45, and one with assets of $158,000 had charges of $227.50. A recent estate of $1,000,000 paid Register's charges of $446.00, while an even larger estate, in the amount of $1,800,000, paid charges of the Register of Wills amounting to only $323.50.

Other Probate Costs

There may be, of course, other probate costs not included in the matters discussed here. For example, there are the expenses of obtaining appraisals of items to be included in the inventory of an estate. In an estate which is below federal estate tax proportions ($60,000) there may be appraisal costs. Maryland law permits the personal representative himself to make the appraisal of corporate stocks listed on any national or regional exchange and, also, any debts owed to the decedent, including bonds and notes. Other items such as real property and tangible personal property may be appraised by the official Orphans' Court appraisers or by such qualified and disinterested appraisers as the personal representative may employ.

In estates of estate tax proportions, the expenses of appraisals are really not costs of probate (although they are properly deductible in determining the net probate estate for inheritance tax and distribution purposes) because these appraisals are necessary in any event for the purpose of preparing the federal estate tax return—*whether or not there is any probate.* These costs, obviously, depend on the nature of the assets to be appraised and the expertise of the appraiser employed by the personal representative; and, while the personal representative will always be interested in obtaining an appraisal at the lowest reasonable cost, nevertheless, at the same time, he will also have in mind the necessity of obtaining an appraisal made by such a competent and disinterested expert, in such detail and sufficiently well documented that the appraisal will withstand the Internal Revenue agent's onslaught at the time of the audit of the return.

Maryland law requires a personal representative, upon his appointment, to publish a notice in a newspaper of general circulation in the county once a week for three successive weeks announcing his appointment and address and notifying creditors of the estate to present their claims. The purpose of this notice, of course, is to give all interested persons, heirs, legatees and creditors an opportunity to know of the existence of the decedent's estate and the names and addresses of those who are handling its administration. Interested parties, then, can object to the appointment of the personal representatives if they have reason to do so and creditors may know to whom and within what period of time they may present their claims. Newspaper charges for this notice currently run between $27 and $30. The statute also requires the Register of Wills to give personal notice of the appointment of the personal representatives to all heirs and legatees by "registered or certified mail, postage prepaid, return receipt requested * * * with delivery restricted to the addressee," for the purpose of making it even more certain that information with respect to the appointment of the personal representatives is made known to all heirs and legatees. It is obvious, therefore, that the postage expenses to satisfy these notices will be proportionately greater for an estate where the will makes provision for many legatees than for the estate where only a few beneficiaries are named in the will. All such personal notices, however, may be waived in writing and if so waived those expenses will be eliminated.

Trust Administration

Where a trust is created under a will, the trustee takes over the trust administration when assets of the estate are delivered to the trustee by the personal representative pursuant to the probate court's approval of an administration account providing for such distribution. The distribution may occur either as a preliminary distribution of the estate, provided for in an interim first or second administration account, or as a final distribution as a result of a final administration account approved by the Orphans' Court. In Maryland, supervision or control of the administration of a testamentary trust is *not* retained by the Orphans' Court or any other court, unless the decedent's will provides otherwise or unless the trustee or any beneficiary should petition for supervision under court jurisdiction, in which event such petition is addressed not to the probate court, but to a court of equity. Since, therefore, distribution of an estate, or any portion of it, in trust or not in trust, terminates the probate court's jurisdiction over so much of the assets of the estate as may then be distributed, the costs of probate come to an end at the time distribution is made; and even though the distribution may be made to a trustee in trust, no further *probate* costs will be incurred as a result of this trust or its administration. This is in sharp contrast to the practice of many other states, where court jurisdiction, and consequently costs, fees, etc., continues during the entire existence of a trust.

Trustees' Fees

Subject to the provisions of the will creating the trust and also to the terms of any valid agreement, the fees of a trustee of a trust created under a will are fixed by law (Maryland Code, Article 16, Section 199). While these commissions are not expenses of probate, simply because probate with respect to the trust's assets has now terminated, consideration of the amounts involved is in order since the fees are the direct result of a trust provided for in the decedent's will.

Under the statute, commissions of the trustee are of two types: commissions on income and annual commissions on principal.

Income commissions are as follows:

6% on all income from real estate, ground rents and mortgages collected in each year.

6% on the first $5,000 of all other income collected in each year; 5% on the next $5,000; 4% on the next $10,000; 3% on the next $10,000; and 2% on any excess.

Such commissions are to be paid out of and chargeable against income.

Principal commissions are as follows:

Annual commissions (payable at the end of each year, accounting from the inception of the trust) on the fair value of the principal held in trust at the end of each year, in the following amounts:

1/4 of 1% on the first $250,000
1/8 of 1% on the next $250,000
1/16 of 1% upon any excess.

Such commissions are to be paid out of and chargeable against principal.

As a practical matter, many banks and trust companies insist on an agreement providing for minimum annual commissions before accepting the office of trustee. (The current minimum annual fee in Baltimore is in the neighborhood of $350.) Because of this, in smaller estates economy usually militates against the creation of a trust.

In addition to commissions in accordance with the schedules set forth above, the statute also provides for trustee's commssions on the sale of real or leasehold property and on final distribution of the trust estate or any portion of it. Trustee's commissions for making sales are allowed in accordance with the rates provided by statute or by the courts of equity in the Maryland county in which the property is located. In the absence of special circumstances commissions on final distribution of the trust estate or any portion of it are at the rate of 1/2 of 1% of the value of the principal so distributed.

Occasionally, it may be advisable for the trustee of a trust created by will to employ an attorney to represent him in a legal matter, or in matters relating to the administration of the trust. The services of an attorney would be appropriate, for example, in representing the trustee in tax matters, in cases necessitating an interpretation or construction of the will, in matters relating to questions of distribution of assets, resignation of trustees, appointment of new trustees and other matters. In such cases, the trustee will usually employ the same attorney who handled the estate administration because, among other things, he is the one who will be most familiar with the background of the legal matters involved. In the event that the trustee should employ an attorney to represent him in connection with the trust matters, the attorney's fees will be determined as though the attorney were handling the same kind of legal work for a client who is not a trustee. In other words, the usual ingredients of time involved, skill required, complexity of issues and the degree of success obtained will all be considered. In instances where the attorney's representation of the trustee results in a legal proceeding before a court of equity, fees of counsel for the trustee will be subject to approval by the court having jurisdiction of the case.

What Does a Will Cost?

A will is most likely to cost a minimum of $50. If one's plan of estate distribution is complicated, irrespective of its total value, there may be a fee of several hundred dollars for a will, and the same for a living trust.

Drafting a will providing for a trust, or drafting even a living trust, can be one of the most difficult tasks undertaken by a lawyer. The complexity of present tax laws alone—further complicated by the Tax Reform Act of 1969—makes it necessary for the lawyer to spend infinitely more time keeping up with tax law changes and decisions than was the case in bygone days. A lawyer's office costs have skyrocketed too, so a $25 fee for drafting a will has gone the way of gold and silver coins. The Maryland State Bar Association's Suggested Minimum Fee Schedule does not attempt to list dollar charges for various types of wills. It does, however, indicate that counsel fees for the preparation of wills should be based primarily on the time spent:

> A so-called "simple" will may require many hours of legal time because the testator insists on many conferences and many changes. On the other hand, a "complicated" will may be largely "boiler plate" although taking up many pages.

> Wills containing trust provisions will normally take more time than those that do not, and so the fee should be higher for them. The more complex the provisions, and the greater the tax involvement, the greater the time required.

When a person employs an attorney to prepare a will, he should not be at all embarrassed to inquire about fees. The subject should be discussed frankly so that reasonable arrangements can be made in advance of the preparation of the will. If extensive estate planning services are required in addition to the drafting of instruments, the fee for such services should be based in large part on the time actually spent in such services.

Summary

When the new Maryland statute relating to decedent's estates became effective on January 1, 1970, Maryland had adopted what is probably the finest and most efficient probate administrative system in the United States. With a proper will, probate court costs are minimal, and real savings can be made in death taxes. The commissions of personal representatives can be estimated once the gross value and nature of the estate and probable income and disbursements are known.

In Maryland, both the commissions of personal representatives and attorneys' fees for legal services in connection with the administration of an estate are subject to determination and approval by the Orphans' Court. In addition, those interested in the decedent's estate are given an adequate opportunity to be heard in opposition to the allowance of any proposed attorneys' commissions and fees deemed to be unreasonable. When a testator does not make a proper will, the cost of administering his estate will be higher than if a properly prepared will has been made by an attorney who is naturally familiar with expense-cutting provisions, meaning of legal terms, consequences of legal principles, requirements for executing wills and the necessity for clear and definite language.

A person needing the services of an attorney should not hesitate to discuss with him his fee or any other cost of probate. Substantial savings of probate costs and taxes can be effected by proper planning.

Glossary

adjusted gross estate: used only for federal estate tax purposes. The adjusted gross estate is the value of the decedent's estate for federal tax purposes, figured by subtracting funeral and administrative expenses, debts, and certain other items from the total value of the estate. It is used in calculating the maximum marital deduction, which is one-half of the adjusted gross estate.

appreciation: growth in the fair market value of the property. The term usually refers to an increase due to fluctuation in the market value of the property rather than changes in the property itself (antonym: depreciation).

beneficiary: one who receives property or an interest therein from another; more particularly one for whose benefit a trust is created; one to whom the proceeds of insurance are payable.

decedent: a deceased person. The term is used whether one dies with or without a will.

disposition: transmitting or directing property ownership, as in disposition of property by a person's will.

encumbrance: a claim, lien, charge or liability against property, such as a mortgage.

estate: the entire property owned by a person, whether land or movable property. In the probate context the term refers to all property left by a decedent.

fair market value: the value of property that would be set by an owner willing (but not forced) to sell for cash and a buyer willing (but not forced) to buy for cash, with both buyer and seller knowing all relevant facts. The fair market value of property is intended to be an estimate in value which is fair, economic and reasonable under normal conditions.

grantor: a person who transfers property other than by will (where he would be called "testator") to someone else (known as the "grantee"). The term is generally used to describe the one who transfers property by gift, by sale or by a trust.

holographic will: a will written entirely in the handwriting of the testator.

intestacy: the state of dying without a valid will disposing of a person's property.

intestate: one who dies without a will.

joinder: joining or coupling together; uniting with another person in some legal step or proceeding.

joint tenancy with right of survivorship: generally, ownership of property by two or more persons who have the same interest in the property and own it together; all rights in the property pass to the survivor upon the death of any one joint tenant and ultimately pass to the last survivor. Thus, the interest of a joint tenant is not included in his probate estate when he dies (though it may be in his taxable estate), since he cannot control the disposition of his interest in the property.

legacy: a gift made by will.

legatee: one who receives a gift made by will.

letters testamentary: a document of authority issued to a personal representative by the probate court showing his authority to serve as personal representative.

liquidity: an asset which can be converted into cash easily. For example, stock which can be easily sold has good liquidity; stock which cannot be easily sold has poor liquidity.

personal representative(s): the individual(s) and/or bank(s) appointed by the Orphans' Court to settle an estate.

personalty: property other than real estate is personalty. The term also applies to contract rights.

probate: the procedure for proving to the satisfaction of the probate court that an instrument is the last will and testament of the decedent; also, as used generally, the appointment of a personal representative and the settlement of an estate.

probate estate: that part of a person's gross estate which will pass under and be subject to his will; if he has no will it passes to his closest relatives.

quitclaim deed: the deed intended to transfer whatever interest, if any, the grantor had. This deed is distinguished from a warranty deed, in which the grantor guarantees that he does have a certain interest.

realty: land and mineral interests. This includes buildings located on the land as well as crops and trees growing on the land (synonyms: real estate, real property, immovables).

survivorship account: an account in the name of two or more persons in which the entire amount passes to the survivor or survivors upon the death of one of the owners. The account may be with a company other than a bank.

tenants in common: ownership by two or more persons of the same piece of property in which each has the right to use or occupy the property at the same time with all the other owners. This type of ownership differs from joint tenancy with right of survivorship in that the interest of the deceased owner does not pass to the survivors. Thus, a tenant in common may dispose of his interest by will, and if there is no will, it will be distributed to his closest relatives.

tenants by the entirety: a tenancy with most of the attributes of a joint tenancy with right of survivorship, but the term is only used as between husband and wife jointly owning property, real or personal.

testator: one who has made a will; one who dies leaving a will. The feminine of testator is "testatrix."

trust: a legal arrangement whereby property is transferred to one person for the benefit of another person.

trustee: the person who holds the property in trust for the benefit of another person, who is called the beneficiary.

valuation: the act of ascertaining or estimating the worth of the property.